W9-AWK-013

RENOUNCE, RESIST, REJOICE

RENOUNCE, RESIST, REJOICE

Being Church in the Age of Trump

Michael Coffey

Foreword by Mark Washington

RESOURCE *Publications* • Eugene, Oregon

RENOUNCE, RESIST, REJOICE
Being Church in the Age of Trump

Resource Publications
An Imprint of Wipf and Stock Publishers
199 W. 8th Ave., Suite 3
Eugene, OR 97401

www.wipfandstock.com

PAPERBACK ISBN: 978-1-5326-1911-3
HARDCOVER ISBN: 978-1-4982-4521-0
EBOOK ISBN: 978-1-4982-4520-3

Manufactured in the U.S.A. 10/10/17

For the people of God at
First English Lutheran Church

and

Vision of Hope African Methodist Episcopal Church
in Austin, Texas
with deep gratitude and joyful admiration

Contents

Foreword

THE WEEK OF JUNE 19th will always serve as a personal reminder of significant events. June 19, 1865, marked the day of emancipation of slaves in Texas, or *Juneteenth*, which started the implementation of liberation from the reluctant but defeated Confederate rule of the South. June 17, 2015, marked the horrific day when nine worshipers were killed by an act of racism and hatred during Bible study in Charleston, South Carolina at Emanuel African Methodist Episcopal Church. However, on June 19, 2015, I received a communication addressed to Vision of Hope African Methodist Episcopal Church in Austin, TX (the church I pastor) from Pastor Michael Coffey of First English Lutheran Church, Austin, TX, to express his sympathy for our denomination. That communication served as the beginning of a relationship and fellowship between our two congregations which had been disconnected due to years of gentrification and social indifference.

I knew Michael Coffey was not a typical Lutheran pastor of a congregation with predominantly white, middle-class parishioners. He was comfortable worshiping and preaching in an African-American church, although being easily recognized as "the visitor" in the pew or pulpit. He facilely hosted a community organizing meeting and enjoyed seeing the church sanctuary overflow with standing room only during a meeting to combat racism and unfair treatment of immigrants. He was in the crowd with marchers and protesters at the state capitol in support of women and immigrant rights. It became clear to me that Michael Coffey was determined to be a part of a church that disciples its members to engage in social justice and healing.

His convictions and comfort in engaging "the other" as part of social justice issues is refreshing and goes beyond the notion of operating in the safe bubble of conservative white privilege for which he and his congregation could have chosen to abide. It is refreshing to see someone serve because of spiritual and social conviction and live the meaning of the church, and not just let the church become a place of sanctimonious seclusion, doctrinal diplomacy, and liturgy that lauds itself in religiosity and zealousness in hope of the celestial "pie in the sky" afterlife, while ignoring the many opportunities to be incarnate and relevant to our community.

In this book, Michael Coffey appropriately illustrates what it means to be church triumphant and militant. "Renounce, Resist, Rejoice: Being Church in the Age of Trump" is very timely. The church needed to be church in the age of Washington, Jefferson, Lincoln, Kennedy, Johnson, and Obama; but there is a heightened and more astute and deliberate ecclesiastical presence that is needed in order to remain relevant during the Trump presidency. The church needs to be church despite the political affiliation of its members, and recognize that liberation and justice are not the property of one political party, but are bi-partisan or anti-partisan, and side with those who are advocates of the oppressed and afflicted.

This book skillfully exegetes the events related to the President Obama-Trump transition of power and provides biblical context, church history, theological reflection, and social insight that will help churches, pastors, lay leaders, as well as people outside the faith community, understand how our scripture and sacred traditions can be used as a resource in providing hope, help, and accountability for leaders in government and community. This work is a prophetic proclamation to leaders and people in a nation conceived in liberty, who sometimes need to be reminded of the proposition that all people are created equal. This work awakens and catapults the church into her obligation to speak truth to power and remind those for which it is not self-evident that all people are created equal and endowed by their Creator with certain unalienable Rights, such as Life, Liberty, and the pursuit of Happiness.

—Rev. Dr. Mark Washington, May, 2017
Pastor of Vision of Hope African Methodist Episcopal Church
in Austin, Texas

Preface

IF YOU'RE A CONSERVATIVE and you made it past the title of this short book, thank you. I hope I don't fail you. I hope my very specific and direct criticisms of politicians and government do not sound like a rejection of you or of conservatism as a valid and important voice in the public and church realm. If you're a liberal and you're motivated by the title of this book, I hope I don't completely fail you. I hope my emphasizing issues and struggles that you may share don't make you think that simply being on the left in the political sense is what matters most, and being church is just a nice thing to do in addition to being a voter or an activist. If I do either of these things in these writings, rejecting conservatives or affirming liberals, then I have failed.

> For just as the body is one and has many members, and all the members of the body, though many, are one body, so it is with Christ. For in the one Spirit we were all baptized into one body—Jews or Greeks, slaves or free—and we were all made to drink of one Spirit. Indeed, the body does not consist of one member but of many. (1 Corinthians 12:12–14)

If Paul were writing his letter to the church at Corinth today to a church in, say, Houston or St. Louis, he would certainly add to his list of once-divided peoples—Jews or Greeks, slaves or free—the now deeply divided conservative or liberal, Republican or Democrat. He would arguably seek to help the divided sides understand that, while they may still have differences, they are now united by something else, something more significant and powerful, something mysterious and wonderful. Paul would most surely shudder at a church chopped up into discrete pieces by partisanship and cultural forces. He would, I dare say, preach and plead for a church to know unity deeper than division, and to act according to that Christ-centered oneness.

I confess that I am writing from what can rightly be called a progressive Christian viewpoint. But if my writing (not to mention my preaching, ministry, and leadership) is simply one more part of the divide, one more pull at the fragile threads that hold us together in this time of discord, than I will have failed. I emphasize in these writings issues centered on marginalized and oppressed peoples, and the church's faithful response to them and with them, and to a nation and political system too often adding to their misery rather than alleviating it. I do so not because I want to promote a liberal political agenda, and even less, a Democratic party agenda. I do so because these issues are part of the bedrock of biblical witness, part of the stream of good news that flows through the church's life from Jesus onward.

It is a mistake to make issues of caring for the poor, welcoming the stranger, lifting up the lowly, and siding with the marginalized uniquely liberal issues. They are issues of compassion, and as the community of Christ's embodied compassion, the church seeks to address them faithfully by the Spirit's power. What faithful conservatives and faithful liberals can do together is pursue, discuss, debate, and enact ministries of care for those God cares so deeply for. They may disagree on how to do these things, how government should be involved, how individual responsibility and communal responsibility inter-relate. But there should be no fundamental disagreement that feeding the hungry and caring for the vulnerable and addressing injustice in the world are the church's yoke to bear in Jesus' name.

I responded to the election of Donald Trump as the forty-fifth president of the United States of America by writing theologically, biblically, pastorally, and politically not because I think I have the path to solving our current deep divide, or because I think there is some easy path to solving our nation's problems. I surely don't. I responded to this historic moment by writing because I think the church matters, and the Gospel message it bears for the world matters. It matters not in some incidental way. It matters in a profound way.

This may be the most unpopular thing I write in this book: Being church matters deeply. Being church today in our liminal moment matters in ways some of us have not felt before, or at least not for a long time. Here again, I hope I am speaking beyond conservative and liberal viewpoints. The church matters, and for conservatives that can be a problem if the individual and his or her relationship with God and the marketplace are all one should care about. The church matters, and for liberals that can be a problem if there is nothing to hope and trust in beyond the political process and the material world. The church matters because it embodies the love of Christ in the flesh so that somewhere in this world, the incarnate love of God can be encountered and trusted.

In Paul's letter to the church in Philippi, he addresses near the end some kind of division or argument. He seems to feel it is urgent to resolve a dispute between two women leaders in the community, or at least find a way to be united even as they disagree.

> Therefore, my brothers and sisters, whom I love and long for, my joy and crown, stand firm in the Lord in this way, my beloved. I urge Euodia and I urge Syntyche to be of the same mind in the Lord. Yes, and I ask you also, my loyal companion, help these women, for they have struggled beside me in the work of the gospel, together with Clement and the rest of my co-workers, whose names are in the book of life. Rejoice in the Lord always; again I will say, Rejoice. Let your gentleness be known to everyone. The Lord is near. Do not worry about anything, but in everything by prayer and supplication with thanksgiving let your requests be made known to God. And the peace of God, which surpasses all understanding, will guard your hearts and your minds in Christ Jesus. (Philippians 4:1–7)

It is my hope that as the church lives out its baptismal calling by renouncing all that opposes love of God and neighbor, and by resisting all that draws us away from this costly love for an easier life, we will together rejoice in the good news of Christ. We can disagree about many things, and be of the same mind in the Lord, rejoicing that in such mysterious love we are, perhaps more than we even desire, united as one.

—Michael Coffey, June 2017

Introduction

As I write this book reflecting on the need for the church to be faithful in new and urgent ways as we begin the Trump presidency, I am keenly aware that at any moment, it may become irrelevant. As each scandal and tweet coming from the White House potentially brings us closer and closer to an early end for the Trump presidency, it appears as if I might not finish this before his term is done. And it's only the first one hundred days. But I am writing anyway. An early end to the Trump presidency, for whatever reason, would not change the importance of addressing where we are as a nation. It would not change the need to address where we are as a church facing tests of faithfulness like we have not known for decades. And whether President Trump is in office or not, something called Trumpism has been unleashed, and it will not simply go away when the man himself goes away. Something that lives barely beneath the surface of American life, and something quite dark, has been revealed, or revealed once again, and cannot be ignored or normalized.

About a week after the inauguration of Donald Trump as the forty-fifth president of the United States, and in particular after the unsupported claims that the Trump inaugural had an attendance greater than the first inaugural of President Obama (photographic images seemed to render this claim ludicrous), and after the first lashing of the press by Sean Spicer (it was not a press conference, as he did not take any questions), and significantly, after the original executive order known as "the Muslim Ban," I posted a status update on Facebook: *There is not enough whiskey in Ireland to get me through the next four years.*

I do enjoy a fine Irish whiskey. I am not driven to drink in excess, though it does seem for many that an evening dram can be a slight balm for the news of the day. I meant this Facebook post, of course, as a humorous way to reflect on what was happening. The daily crises and unprecedented actions emanating from the White House were quickly becoming exhausting. Many friends liked the post and commented in appropriately humorous ways. One Facebook friend, a woman who I grew up with in my hometown from second grade until high school graduation, but whom I have not had contact with since high school until Facebook reconnected us a few year ago, posted this: *I hope you don't have any Republicans in your church.*

Of course, I do have Republicans in my church, even though the congregation I serve is mostly progressive theologically and politically. But there are a good number of faithful, thoughtful church members who tend to vote Republican. Those who have talked about it told me they could not and did not vote for Donald Trump, but some may have voted for him and are not speaking out about their choice.

The exchange with the Facebook friend continued. She implied that I was insulting Republicans in my church or any church because of my criticisms of Donald Trump. I pointed out that I was not criticizing voters. I was not looking for a partisan divide in the church, nor a political argument on Facebook. None of that interests me much.

I said that I was speaking to issues, and in particular, issues affecting people's lives, especially vulnerable people who were feeling afraid and unsure of their futures. I said I was holding our newly elected leader accountable for his words and actions. I also said that when we come together as church, we do not label ourselves as "Republican" or "Democrat" or any other partisan label. We come together as baptized members of Christ seeking to be faithful to our calling and wrestling with hard questions of how to do that today. I ended my comments by stating that as a called pastor in the Lutheran church, speaking out for the poor and vulnerable and against injustice is in my job description. It is not a partisan act. It is a public act of speaking God's Word on behalf of those who are suffering.

I share this exchange because this book might appear to be a partisan work, about Democrats and Republicans and which party God favors, or something like that. This is not a partisan book. It is, however, a political book. Politics in the strict sense is the process of ordering our lives together in the public realm. The church is political (but not partisan) because it is called to speak to issues of our public lives, the common good, and how we order our social, economic, legal, and communal relationships to benefit all and witness to God's mercy and justice. In particular, the church is called to witness in public to how the machinations of human power are subject to sin and corruption, and leave people behind. For those people who are left behind and have little power or voice in the public realm, the church speaks and works for justice and mercy in the way of Jesus.

+++

The election party started off with excitement and a bit of suppressed jubilation. This was our fourth presidential election party at our house, and we have always enjoyed gathering together with friends to share the once-every-four-years' experience of electing a president. Whether or not the person we voted for wins, it is exhilarating to gather together with good friends of various political persuasions, share food and drinks, and watch the electoral college count unfold. We typically make a poster-sized map of the United States and color in the red and blue states as they are called. Our children grew up participating in this basic expression of democracy by helping color in the states and keep count. Some years, our candidate won and we celebrated. Other years, our candidate lost and we licked our wounds and accepted it and moved on.

This year's party was something entirely different. Most of us were either exuberant in our support for Hillary Clinton and moved by the thought of electing the first woman president, or had begrudgingly voted for her because the alternative was unthinkable and unacceptable. I had been following the polls and the likely electoral outcomes for months. My daily visits to the 270towin.com and realclearpolitics.com web sites had me feeling like a confident expert. I had assured everyone that while it could be close, it was clear that Hillary Clinton would win the presidency, and the 18 months of listening to Donald Trump's racism, misogyny, anti-Muslim bigotry, and general sophistry when it came to governmental realities, would be over. I had mixed batches of *El Presidente* cocktails, a tasty mixture of rum, vermouth, orange Curaçao, and grenadine, joking about the Trumpish orange color as a bad omen.

Then, one by one the states that were sure to give Clinton an electoral victory went for Trump. At first my response was to comfort everyone at the party: *She can still win without Florida.* And then more quick calculations in my head about what the bare minimum states were that she needed to win. And then the bare minimum states went for Trump. A sinking feeling overcame everyone as we watched the newscasters of various channels, themselves in disbelief, make it clear that Donald Trump was the forty-fifth president. No one on television exhibited this more clearly than Stephen Colbert, whose live episode of *The Late Show* had clearly been planned for a Clinton win. As the news rolled in on the electoral inevitability of a Trump win, Colbert became subdued and deflated, and he struggled for words. There was little comedy. That's how the party felt.

I have been voting since the presidential election of 1984. Some years my candidate won. Some years my candidate lost. What happened on November 8, 2016 felt nothing like those experiences when my candidate lost. This had nothing to do with party or voting or being on the winning or losing side. It suddenly felt like our nation had taken a dark turn that would degrade women, threaten immigrants and refugees and Muslims, throw millions of people into the uncertain and frightful reality of losing their health insurance, and diminish the voting rights and civil rights of African Americans. There is more I could say here about all the people who had been demeaned, threatened, and sidelined by the Trump campaign. And now, it looked like those nightmarish policies and attitudes would come to power.

The next morning, I woke up in a fuzzy dysphoria unable to make sense of what had happened. I quickly shrugged off my own self-concern as best I could. I realized there were many who were so much more affected by this than I was because their lives were now threatened. I was a relatively comfortable and safe white male who could coast along and feel little personal change in my life, save for the fact that I still had a conscience and a moral compass. I decided I had to stay home and write something in response to the election, rather than drive into the church and try to start a normal work day. I had to find some way to speak to the church and all those in fear, and therefore to myself, to find a way to respond to the election results that felt so crushing to so many. I had to find a way to rise above despair and disbelief and face this new reality head on.

I wrote *A Pastoral Letter after the Election of Donald Trump* and posted it on my blog by late morning, and then shared it on Facebook. It hit a nerve. Before I knew it, I had 5,000 page views and people commenting and sharing the post over the next few days. People thanked me. People shared their struggle to face the election results. People were looking for some way through the uncertainty. If my words helped in any way to move forward and find a way to keep living in hope, love, and light, then I was going to write and write some more. Some of these pieces were written in the immediate aftermath of the election, some in the following months, and some are older works of mine I have rethought in light of our current political crisis.

I write this book not as a partisan, but as a person of faith and a pastor who feels called to help find a way through challenging and confusing times. If you are a person of Christian faith, I write this so we can wrestle together with the question of how to be faithful. Whether you voted for Trump, or Clinton, or a third-party candidate, or didn't vote or can't vote, we need to talk together about how to be church in the age of Trump and beyond.

I am risking being provocative so we can have that conversation and seek faithfulness together. No matter who we support in government, or what political party we align with, as people of faith, baptized into Christ, we are called to seek together the way of the kingdom, the good news of God, in this world and in our time. We are called to work out together how the cross, how Jesus' solidarity with all who suffer, is embodied in our own lives. How do we do that in the age of Trump? How do we do that in any age? Let's commit ourselves to this hard work together now like never before.

Part One

RENOUNCE

Then Nebuchadnezzar in furious rage commanded that Shadrach, Meshach, and Abednego be brought in; so they brought those men before the king. Nebuchadnezzar said to them, "Is it true, O Shadrach, Meshach, and Abednego, that you do not serve my gods and you do not worship the golden statue that I have set up? Now if you are ready when you hear the sound of the horn, pipe, lyre, trigon, harp, drum, and entire musical ensemble to fall down and worship the statue that I have made, well and good. But if you do not worship, you shall immediately be thrown into a furnace of blazing fire, and who is the god that will deliver you out of my hands?" Shadrach, Meshach, and Abednego answered the king, "O Nebuchadnezzar, we have no need to present a defense to you in this matter. If our God whom we serve is able to deliver us from the furnace of blazing fire and out of your hand, O king, let him deliver us. But if not, be it known to you, O king, that we will not serve your gods and we will not worship the golden statue that you have set up." (Daniel 3:13–18)

For the grace of God has appeared, bringing salvation to all, training us to renounce impiety and worldly passions, and in the present age to live lives that are self-controlled, upright, and godly, while we wait for the blessed hope and the manifestation of the glory of our great God and Savior, Jesus Christ. He it is who gave himself for us that he might redeem us from all iniquity and purify for himself a people of his own who are zealous for good deeds. Declare these things; exhort and reprove with all authority. Let no one look down on you. (Titus 2:11–15)

A Pastoral Letter after the Election of Donald Trump

DEAR BROTHERS AND SISTERS in Christ at First English Lutheran Church and all who belong to the body of Christ,

Grace and peace to you in the name of Jesus, our brother and Lord, the man of peace, the incarnation of God's love for all.

The election of Donald Trump as the 45th president of the United States may strike each of us in different ways. Some of you may have voted for him and are pleased. You may feel that the brokenness of our politics and economy now have a chance to be mended and work better for those who have been left out. Let us hope, pray, and work together for those good ends.

Others may have voted for Hillary Clinton and are disappointed, and possibly quite upset. You may feel that this loss is a shock, and is a significant shift away from your hopes of forming a nation where more and more people have full participation in society with mutual respect and rights ensured. Let us hope, pray, and work together for those good ends still.

In the Gospel of Luke, Jesus gave something like an inaugural address at the very beginning of his ministry and his earthly reign as the prince of peace and the embodiment of divine mercy. The text goes like this:

> When he came to Nazareth, where he had been brought up, he went to the synagogue on the sabbath day, as was his custom. He stood up to read, and the scroll of the

> prophet Isaiah was given to him. He unrolled the scroll and found the place where it was written:
>
> > "The Spirit of the Lord is upon me,
> > because he has anointed me
> > to bring good news to the poor.
> > He has sent me to proclaim release to the captives
> > and recovery of sight to the blind,
> > to let the oppressed go free,
> > to proclaim the year of the Lord's favor."
>
> And he rolled up the scroll, gave it back to the attendant, and sat down. The eyes of all in the synagogue were fixed on him. Then he began to say to them, "Today this scripture has been fulfilled in your hearing." (Luke 4:16–21)

I am aware that at this moment, many are responding to the election with anxiety and fear. I am thinking specifically about:

- Muslim Americans who fear they will be oppressed and face greater hatred
- Mexican Americans and other Latinos who fear their family members may be rounded up en masse and deported
- Women who fear that language that normalizes sexual assault will become acceptable
- LGBTQ persons who fear losing their rights as full citizens
- African Americans who fear a growing backlash against the first African-American president and the further eroding of voter rights
- Persons with health insurance gained through the Affordable Care Act who fear that within months they will no longer have health insurance.
- Others who have been listening to offensive words that degrade and reject their full personhood coming from the man who will be the next president

There are more I could list. Whether you are supportive of the election results or opposed, we can all keep in mind that many people will now live with legitimate fear and anxiety about their well-being and their families' futures.

The beginning of Jesus' public life laid out a vision and a hope that we need to hear now. It is one of care for the poor, the oppressed, and the hurting. It is a message of liberation and release. It is a deep trust in the work of the Spirit to bring about what no human institution can bring about: The kingdom of God's reign of love and mercy for all.

People of faith are called to shape and support human institutions like government to reflect the values and visions of God's reign. But they are never called to put their ultimate trust and hope in those institutions. They are called to a faith that rises above the limited and deeply flawed world that people can create, even as they work within, for, and when necessary, against those institutions.

We are a people called to a life of loving our neighbors, caring for the least, working for a world of justice with mercy, and most of all, placing all our trust in one who created us out of love and called us to be love in a world longing for and fighting against God's love. It's a hard calling, one symbolized by the cross of Jesus, one known throughout history in the lives of humble servants and the blood of martyrs.

Beloved, no matter how you voted, this is how we must live together: loving our neighbors, caring for the least, working for a world of justice with mercy, and placing our trust in God alone. Our call is the same now as it was yesterday, though for some of us, it may feel more urgent and daunting. So be it. We follow Christ Jesus, who lived the costly love of God in all its fullness no matter the cost, who died for that love to be revealed through powerlessness and humility, and who rose to be the great, divine "yes" to all of this world's "no" to God's reign.

Work with me, brothers and sisters, in being the people of light and love, now more than ever. We do not do this work alone. We have the Spirit of the Lord upon us through baptism and grace, and the presence of the risen Lord Jesus, who walks this stumbling path with us all the way to the end. And the end is not your worst fear, but your greatest hope, and something even greater than that.

Peace to all in Christ.

Your Baptism Is Calling You

The Church in Trying Times

Written between the election and the inauguration

We are living in trying times. The election of Donald Trump has many living in fear, anxiety, and expectation that their lives may be in danger or their families may be ripped apart. This is not a normal reaction to a presidential election. This is not persons upset because their candidate lost. This is a reasonable reaction to the eighteen months of racist, xenophobic, and misogynist speech of the candidate himself. As we have seen in the rise of hate speech and crimes, whether or not Donald Trump himself believes the things he says, he has stirred up, empowered, and emboldened those who do to act out in hate, intimidation, and violence.

More than that, president-elect Trump has appointed Steve Bannon as his chief strategist. Bannon is a man well known to be a supporter of the alt-right movement, which is blatantly racist. His former job as the head of Breitbart News gave him a ready platform to promote these beliefs, and Breitbart infamously has. We now have a white nationalist in a high position of power in the upcoming administration. We now have the authority and power of the White House making racism, xenophobia, and misogyny normal, acceptable, and powerful.

Church, your baptism is calling you.

In the ancient tradition of Christian baptism, the message is very clear: By going into the water, you are dying to an old life, and rising to a new one. The old life? That's the life of sin, self-centeredness, lack of love for God and neighbor. The new life? Love, love for all, love for the other, the love of Christ mysteriously finding its expression in the flesh through you.

Baptism is about the paschal mystery of death and resurrection as the only path to new life. It comes through the death and resurrection of Christ, but it is now the death and resurrection of the baptized person. Early Christians made baptism a highly significant ritual. The initiation process, architecture, and rituals all said this is a life-and-death matter. Some ancient baptismal fonts had steps leading down into the water, and steps leading out the other side. They speak of drowning and dying, and then rising to a new life. Some early Christian fonts were round, symbolizing a womb of rebirth. Some were octagonal, speaking to the "eighth day" of resurrection, as Christians thought of it, a new day of creation where the old has passed away and in the resurrection of Christ, the new has appeared.

In the ancient baptismal tradition, one important thing must happen before the baptism. The baptismal candidate is asked three vital questions. And after each question, the candidate says: I renounce them. Here are the questions:

Do you renounce the devil and all the forces that defy God?

I renounce them.

Do you renounce the powers of this world that rebel against God?

I renounce them.

Do you renounce the ways of sin that draw you from God?

I renounce them.

This is a bold statement that the baptismal candidate is making, and the church is making with her. Something must be renounced in order to have new life in Christ. I think the rubrics here should say: *Shouted with every fiber of one's being: I renounce them!*

In some ancient traditions, this renunciation is ritualized by facing west, the direction of the setting sun, the way of darkness. Facing that darkness, facing evil, the triple renunciation is spoken boldly, as if to speak directly into the face of evil and say, nope, I'm done with you. Then, the candidate faces east, the direction of the rising sun, the way of light, and confesses faith in Christ.

And then the baptism, the plunging into the waters of death and resurrection, the joining of one's life to Christ indelibly, the rebirth. After the baptism in many traditions, the newly baptized, still wet and fresh, is handed a lit candle and given this charge that comes from Jesus in the Sermon on the Mount in Matthew:

> Let your light so shine before others
> so they may see your good works
> and glorify your Father in heaven. (Matthew 5:16)

Forget cute babies and frilly gowns. This is serious business. This is rejection of evil to its face, and embracing of God's love and the way of love Jesus embodied. Christians call this baptismal ritual a sacrament, meaning it is an action of God to transform us from the old to the new. It is something hardly believable, and yet believing it can change your entire life.

We are living in trying times. The legitimizing of hatred and persecution of others is dangerous. We know where these things can go from the frightening lessons of history. Renouncing evil and hatred and sin and all that draws us from love of God and neighbor is not a one-time thing. We are called back to it daily, just as we are called daily to hear and trust the good news of Christ.

Church, your baptism is calling you. Renounce what you have already been called to renounce. Do it loudly and robustly and with exclamation points and every fiber of your being. Die again to the old life that keeps coaxing us backwards. Rise again to the new life of love in Christ's name. Let your light shine in the darkness. Let others see your good works. Give glory to God, who loved you, called you, and made you new.

Your baptism is calling you. Renounce. Die and rise. Shine with light and love. The light shines in the darkness, and the darkness cannot overcome it.

Thanks be to God.

#NotMyPresident? #NotMyKing!

Sermon for Christ the King Sunday

Here's a tough and tricky question for you: Who is your president? Emotions are running strong in this post-election moment. Many are tempted to speak and tweet #notmypresident. It happened with Obama. It's happening now with Trump. The problem is, in a democratic system we agree that whoever wins the election is president for all of us, not just those who voted for him or her. And when we say they are our president we say we have the right to hold them accountable and to make sure they are being president for everyone.

It's a bit different in the Bible, though. We hear Jeremiah speaking about the king of Judah, who was a puppet king put in place by Nebuchadnezzar after Judah was conquered and many deported to Babylon.

> The days are surely coming, says the Lord,
> when I will raise up for David a righteous Branch,
> and he shall reign as king and deal wisely,
> and shall execute justice and righteousness in the land.
> In his days Judah will be saved and Israel will live in safety.
> And this is the name by which he will be called:
> "The Lord is our righteousness." (Jeremiah 23:5–6)

There's a subtle trick going on in the text, which is only seen in the Hebrew. The puppet king put in place by Nebuchadnezzar at the time Jeremiah was writing was named Zedekiah, which means

The Lord is righteousness. But in Jeremiah's prophetic speech, he says God will put in place our true king and his name will be Zedekenu: *The Lord is our righteousness.* When Jeremiah says the king will not be Zedekiah but Zedakenu, he is making a verbal jab at Nebuchadnezzar's terrible rule over Judah. Zedekiah is #NotMyKing.

Christianity has always been a political faith. Not in the sense of putting our ultimate trust in one party, or leader, or philosophy of government, or economic system. Christianity has always been political because we make a confession of who our true Lord, king, ruler, authority, governor, president is: Jesus is Lord! This is what always got early Christians into trouble. They confessed it loudly and boldly in public: Jesus is Caesar! Jesus is emperor! Jesus is president! and no one else. Any other authority is secondary at best, is #NotMyKing, and does not ever override the authority of God's reign in our lives through Christ Jesus.

The key thing to understand in this radical Christian claim is what kind of ruler, king, president Jesus is. It might be surprising that our Gospel text for Christ the King Sunday is the story of Jesus' crucifixion in Luke, but Luke says something incredibly important here. Everyone is shouting to Jesus: Save yourself! Everyone wants Jesus to use his power to save himself, either to prove who he is, or so they could get something out of it along with Jesus.

And what becomes clear by the end of the story is Jesus refuses to save himself. Jesus refuses to save himself because that is the problem with this whole human mess: people constantly trying to save themselves, to use what they have to protect only themselves, to make life work out for a small vision about us only and nothing larger like the vision of God's kingdom.

Here's what is so powerful about this text: Jesus saves us by not saving himself, by reigning in the world through powerlessness, by confronting human institutional power with the power of God's love which always looks foolish in the capitals of power, but always reveals divine love for those open to seeing it.

All of God's reign is revealed in the cross of Christ, not when we look up, like we do at tall capitols and skyscrapers and football stadiums and cathedrals, but when we look down; not when we pursue power, but when we serve; not when we try to fix everything to go our way, but when we show compassion for those whom the world does not go their way; not when we win, but when we gather with all the losers who know God is their hope.

One of the ways we show this in the church is in the ritual of bowing at the cross. We bow at the cross when it processes by or when we enter the sacred worship space because we honor him who reigns from down low, not from on high. We lift him up visually and prominently among us so that his lowliness can be fully seen, not so he can rule over others like a despot, but so his reign of compassion can be proclaimed. We lift him up, not because he reigns from on high, but because he reigns from down low, where the poor and suffering are, where we are when we give up lifting up ourselves.

The questions and struggles for the church are always: Does it matter if we believe this and live it out? How do we live it out in our world that worships human power and domination? It is a struggle the church has not always been faithful to. History is filled with the church's failure to praise Jesus as Lord and king.

Dietrich Bonhoeffer is the well-known Lutheran pastor who lived in Germany during the rise of Hitler and National Socialism. He spoke against the church of his time, the church we would call the Lutheran Church, which they call the Evangelical Church, but started to call the German Church, a church of nationalism for Germans only. Bonhoeffer pondered this text from Second Corinthians:

> but he said to me, "My grace is sufficient for you, for power is made perfect in weakness." So I will boast all the more gladly of my weaknesses, so that the power of Christ may dwell in me. (2 Corinthians 12:9)

In interpreting this text for his own time, Bonhoeffer wrote in a sermon:

> Christianity stands or falls with its revolutionary protest against violence, arbitrariness, and pride of power, and

> with its plea for the weak. Christians are doing too little to make these points clear rather than too much. Christendom adjusts itself far too easily to the worship of power. Christians should give more offense, shock the world far more, than they are doing now. Christians should take a stronger stand in favor of the weak, rather than considering first the possible right of the strong. (from *The Collected Sermons of Dietrich Bonhoeffer.* Edited by Isabel Best. Fortress Press: Minneapolis. 2012)

The church living in times of injustice and under empires that work against the kingdom of God, still follows the way of Jesus. We don't fight back, we love back, even when that love looks like a fight for justice.

In 2004 Victor Yushchenko ran for the presidency of Ukraine. The incumbent prime minister Viktor Yanukovych and his ruling party, the Party of Regions, opposed him and worked to make sure he was not elected. They nearly killed him by poisoning, but he still ran for president.

On November 24, 2004, as the election unfolded, Yushchenko was in the lead. The ruling party controlled the state-run media, however, so they reported: *Ladies and gentlemen, we announce that the challenger Victor Yushchenko has been decisively defeated.*

The television channel made use of a sign language interpreter during the broadcast. Natalie Dmitruk appeared in the lower corner of the screen signing the news as it was being reported by the speaking newscaster. As the lies about who was winning were being spoken on air, Dmitruk refused to translate them. Instead, she signed to the deaf community: *I'm addressing all the deaf citizens of Ukraine. They are lying and I'm ashamed to translate those lies. Yushchenko is our president.*

The only persons who received the truth that night were the hearing impaired and those who knew their language. They began to act. They contacted their friends and told them the results were a lie. Soon, the truth began to spread and a movement started. In the coming weeks, the Orange Revolution began, and by the end of the political turmoil, the truth had won and Yushchenko was declared the winner.

Who can interpret the signs of truth today? The cross is our sign language. At times only we can understand it. Jesus is Lord. Jesus is king. Jesus is president. The church speaks and acts in ways that make his gentle rule all the more visible in the world today. The church speaks this good news for all longing to hear it, and often when some other false news is being broadcast.

How will we follow Christ Jesus today? How will his reign override all the other powers for us? We must figure that out today in new ways. But it will surely look like Jesus on the cross, the one we lift up, because he reigns from down low, with mercy, where the poor and suffering are, and where we are when we give up trying to save ourselves.

A People Living by Hope

One Candle Will Have to Be Enough

It is tempting to live by despair. The political shifts toward anger, racism, xenophobia, and nationalism have created a mood of anguish for many. Just at the moment when winter is approaching and the days are getting longer and darker, it feels like our society is growing darker, too. People who live by faith in the coming kingdom of God inaugurated in Jesus, people who seek a world of justice, reconciliation, unity in diversity, can feel at times as if we have taken several giant leaps backwards. It is tempting to live by despair.

The season of Advent, a favorite time of year for a contemplative spirit such as my own, is a time to turn our attention away from despair and toward hopefulness. It calls to mind the coming of Christ in the past, an event of great expectation, to shape how we see and trust the coming of Christ in the future, and even the coming of Christ into every now. It is always an arrival of grace, an incarnation of love, a reign of mercy, and a kingdom of justice. Advent says: We are a people who live by hope, even when we don't. And hope is a renunciation of the hopeless ways of the world that oppose God's ways.

In Scripture, we hear the prophet Isaiah speak of a time to come. We can surmise that he was speaking to a people living in despair. War, economic injustice, fear, and doubt were all too familiar to them. And into that moment and those lives, Isaiah speaks of a day to come when God will be the one who arbitrates disputes between nations and between peoples. Because God is just and righteous, arguments will be settled fairly. Therefore, there will be no need for war or instruments of war. They will be pointless and a waste of metal and wood. They will be repurposed into farming implements to feed people and give life. Of this time to come, Isaiah says:

> For out of Zion shall go forth instruction,
> and the word of the Lord from Jerusalem.
> He shall judge between the nations,
> and shall arbitrate for many peoples;
> they shall beat their swords into plowshares,
> and their spears into pruning hooks;
> nation shall not lift up sword against nation,
> neither shall they learn war any more. (Isaiah 2:3b–4)

We are living in a time of great arguments about the way we should go. The disputatious political parties seem unable to judge between their differences themselves. Common citizens struggle to articulate and discuss the deep longing and sadness they feel at the state of the world, and quickly devolve into argument, name calling, and divisiveness. If ever there was a time we needed an arbitrator, and a holy and divine one at that, it is now. Our weapons are still sharp and deemed useful, weapons of words, political power, hatred, segregation into like-mindedness, and nationalism.

On the first Sunday of Advent, many churches and individuals perform a ritual. On a wreath that includes four candles, only one candle is lit. It sits there, giving some light, but next to three unlit candles. It's a ritual that is visual and demonstrative of this hard truth: That day we dream of, that kingdom we long for, that world of peace and justice is not here yet. It is a promised day, but one we still only hold a promissory note for, a rain check. On this day, as far as we can tell, we must live by hope, hope rooted in a deep trust in God's promises, hope that must learn the painful discipline of patience in the face of struggle.

The patience and hope of people of faith is not a passive and do-nothing thing. Our faith dares us to believe that we are part of

God's movement in the world, a cell in the body of Christ straining and lurching towards that great day we await, at times by inches, and at times by miles. But today, during real trials and suffering and antagonism towards God's reign of peace, one candle is all we get.

In the great Gospel song by Andraé Crouch, *Soon and Very Soon*, we sing of the day when we are going to see the king, the one who settles our disputes both national and personal so our weapons can be repurposed to grow food and give life. It is by great, audacious faith that we sing of that day coming soon, and very soon, and even sing *Hallelujah!* We know it may be far off, but it is at least one day closer and sooner. We live by a great, hopeful faith that nothing, not even the dark days, can crush.

During the first week of Advent with live with just one candle lit, and three reminding us of the darkness. This is a poignant symbol of what it often means to live with faith any season of the year. One candle is lit giving slim light, and many more unlit speak of waiting for greater illumination. But one candle, the candle of hope that renounces hopelessness, will have to be enough.

Hey Liberal, Progressive, Conservative, Traditional Christians

It Starts with You.

It is tempting during a time of divisiveness to blame others for the problems we face. It is even more tempting with the rise of a demagogic president who has played on the fears and selfish desires of the people to blame others for what is going wrong. I admit it. I have spent a lot of time and energy thinking: *What is wrong with those people?* And I have been more than willing to provide my own answers.

But then during the Advent season, which has perhaps never been better timed for the cultural and political moment, at least not in my lifetime, we hear about John the Baptist. I admit right up front, John is one of my biblical fascinations. He is a wild man archetype. He is a mentor to Jesus. He is a much-needed ice pick of a voice breaking through the frozen souls of the liberals and the conservatives of his day. John is introduced in Matthew like this:

> In those days John the Baptist appeared in the wilderness of Judea, proclaiming, "Repent, for the kingdom of heaven has come near." This is the one of whom the prophet Isaiah spoke when he said,
>
> "The voice of one crying out in the wilderness:
> 'Prepare the way of the Lord,
> make his paths straight.'"

> Now John wore clothing of camel's hair with a leather belt around his waist, and his food was locusts and wild honey. Then the people of Jerusalem and all Judea were going out to him, and all the region along the Jordan, and they were baptized by him in the river Jordan, confessing their sins. (Matthew 3:1–6)

He is rough and uninhibited. He is attractive and fearsome in the way a lion is, untamed and roaring in strong beauty. He speaks to the heart because he goes straight to it without playing around with social, religious, or political conventions. He calls people to a new life, a life of getting ready for God's new and wonderful thing, a life that begins only through the portal of repentance.

You could be tempted to think, when you hear John's wilderness scowl, he is speaking to someone else. Probably the people you disagree with. Or perhaps people you agree with but who are just not quite getting with the program. So listen to John speak to the very folks who think that way:

> But when he saw many Pharisees and Sadducees coming for baptism, he said to them, "You brood of vipers! Who warned you to flee from the wrath to come? Bear fruit worthy of repentance. Do not presume to say to yourselves, 'We have Abraham as our ancestor'; for I tell you, God is able from these stones to raise up children to Abraham. Even now the ax is lying at the root of the trees; every tree therefore that does not bear good fruit is cut down and thrown into the fire. (Matthew 3:7–10)

The Pharisees and the Sadducees were the liberal and conservative parties of their day, at least within Jewish life. They disagreed with each other. They blamed each other for whatever was going wrong. They argued over whose side God was on. They probably came out to see the fascinating John assuming that the other ones were going to repent, be baptized, change their ways, and become like them. They wanted to see that and feel a little better about themselves.

And John says to the whole sorry mess: You all need to repent! You all need to look at how you are part of the problem! None of you escapes this hard path because you're part of the "right" party or group or ideology, or because you voted one way or another! It's you! It starts with you!

And then people humbled themselves, opened up about their own failings more than their opponents', went down deep into the water, and came out with a new start. They were ready to embrace the new, open reality of God's kingdom breaking in because they had given up on the old, closed reality of their own small minds and self-righteousness.

One of the great gifts of the church is the ritual and discipline of confession of sins, repentance, pronouncement of forgiveness, and the chance to walk the path of life anew. It is a source of great hope that there are communities of faith willing to confess their own errors more than they accuse others of theirs. It might be the only thing that makes it possible for God to work newness among us and in the world.

What to do now as the church responds to a difficult time with the potential for a rise in hatred, racism, nationalism, fear, and blaming others? Let the wildness and cry of John reach us. Confess. Repent. Trust forgiveness. Listen to each other with open ears and hearts. Walk anew the path of love in a time of hate.

Prepare the way. It starts with you, with us, here and now beloved, or it might not start anywhere with anyone.

Hey White Church

The Time Has Come

THE MARGIN OF VICTORY for President Trump was slim. He lost the popular vote by the largest margin ever. He won the electoral college by a sizeable margin, though not the historically huge win he has often claimed. But in the key swing states that made the difference in the electoral count, his margins of victory were small, just tens of thousands of voters. The election could easily have gone another way.

All the polling data from the presidential election show something that, I must admit, I wish were not true. White people elected Donald Trump. Trump won the white vote with 56%. In contrast, he only got 21% of the non-white vote. Looking at specific groups, we see that Trump only got 8% of the Black vote, 28% of the Latino vote, and 27% of the Asian vote.

But these data aren't as important for the church to consider as the data for how various Christians voted. White evangelicals voted for Trump by 81%. White Catholics voted for Trump by 60%. It is not an exaggeration to say not just that white people elected Trump, but that white Christians elected him. What does it mean to say that the white church elected Donald Trump? Does it mean white Christians promote intolerance and bigotry? Does it mean the white church is uncaring about anyone other than whites? Does it mean white Christians are sensing that their social dominance, which lasted for centuries, is nearing an end and they are grabbing after the last thread of power, thinking they can return to a world that has faded long ago? Who knows? Pollsters can't quite agree on what motivated the white vote, let alone the white Christian vote. It would be simplistic to settle on an easy answer, or to claim that each person who voted for Donald Trump agrees with all the hateful rhetoric of his campaign. It might be hard to understand how they do not agree with him while voting for him, but it may very well be something else motivating their voting.

But then again, the time has come for the white church to admit that it has lived a life of white privilege both inside and outside of the church. Even worse, in many times and places throughout our nation's history, the white church has endorsed vocally and tacitly the predominant racist beliefs of our culture. So when an election of such historic significance as the presidential election of 2016 gives us a winning candidate who explicitly promoted racist and discriminatory words and policies, and that candidate is favored by a majority of white Christians and rejected and feared by a majority of Christians of color, it is time to sit up and take notice.

Here's a true confession: During the week after the election, I was feeling ashamed of being white. The words and actions, the fearfulness and self-preserving focus of white culture led to a time in history when non-whites felt more intimidated and afraid for their well-being. I didn't want to be a part of it anymore. I talked with several friends, white and non-white, and was brought to tears trying to figure out: *What the hell is wrong with white people?* Well, this is nothing new of course, and I'm not naïve about the long history of white supremacy in our culture and in the church. But it felt like it had more prominence and power than ever before in my lifetime.

I felt like I had to do something. As a white man, I felt I had to become part of the solution, and not a quiet and passive part of the problem. I could sit comfortably and innocuously in my white male life of relative ease, but that felt sickening to me now. What to do? Not only am I a part of the white church concerned about its faithfulness and its fearful clinging to whatever is left of white power and white supremacy, I am also a white man. Being a white man comes with a burden. It is not Rudyard Kipling's "The White Man's Burden," the supposed problem of how to enforce white supremacy in the world through colonialism. The burden of the white man I speak of is very much the opposite: How to keep seeing and confronting ourselves and our often implicitly assumed but very much asserted privilege, power, and supposed supremacy of being white and being male.

I came up with a big idea, a movement for white men to be a force for good. It seemed a little crazy, but it felt purposeful, and in the palpable urgency following the election, it seemed right to do something rather than nothing. White men needed to stand up together and speak out for the non-white, non-male population in new and powerful ways. I sensed this was fraught with danger. I knew it could be just another way for white men to feel important and in control. But I wrote up the idea anyway, which I share here with some hesitancy.

+++

Let's face it, white men. We had a pretty good run. Well, pretty good for many of us, not so great for women and persons of color. Pretty awful, actually. Still, we had our shot at making the world, and we often made a world that worked well for us. No, not all of us. Lots of white men have struggled and suffered and have been left out of the economy and the places of power. But, in total, we had our shot.

That's mostly over. Sorry to have to break it to you if you haven't realized it, or if you're fearful of accepting it. The white man's world is almost gone, and this may be hard to hear: we think that's a good thing. It might not feel good, it might hurt, but men can deal with hurt. It might look like it's going the other way with the election of Donald Trump as president, but that's just the death rattles of a dying white man's world. That's just the leftover fear of having eight years of a black man in the white house. White men, trust us. It's over.

The thing is, now we have our chance to live as selfless men, men who have something to live for besides ourselves and our own accumulation of power. Men who know that we are called to stand up for others and fight for their well-being in the face of increasing hatred and injustice. People like women, the other half of the world, traumatized by sexual assault and words that make that sound acceptable. People like Muslims and Latino immigrants who fear violence and expulsion. People like African Americans losing their voting rights and facing increasing overt racism. People like the LGBTQ community who feel even more vulnerable now. People like anyone who doesn't live with the social, economic, and political privileges of being white and male, and face obstacles old and new that we have not faced.

The sad thing we must face is, many of the awful things happening to others are done by other white men, the white men whose fear of losing power and control is driving them to blaming others and grabbing whatever power they can. We can be sympathetic to the deep anxiety many white men feel from realizing we will no longer control the world. It's real. It's disorienting. It feels like losing. But we do not need to support, affirm, accept, or tolerate the actions of other white men who harm others through words and deeds because of their fear and anxiety.

We do not need to spend a lot of time feeling defensive about the world we helped make and benefit from still. We do not need to wallow in guilt. Both of those things are about us, and we need to get over making it all about us.

What we can do is this: Stand up. Stand up for others. Stand up for all others who have not benefited from the white man's world but are now just beginning to benefit from a changing world that includes them. We can stand up for women. Stand up for Native Americans. Stand up for our African-American brothers and sisters. Stand up for immigrants and refugees who are vulnerable and desperate for help. Stand up for all who are unable to stand up for themselves, because that's what mature men do.

We can stand up and we can act. That's what men do. We see when and where others need our help, our strength, our power, our selflessness, our courage, our fearlessness, and we stand up and act. Now, don't get us wrong, we aren't now meaning to create a new, separate, empowered white male society, only spinning it as something for the good. We are calling for white men to stand up with women, stand up with persons of color, stand up with others, and use whatever power and privilege we have for their sake.

We also need to listen to whomever it is we feel called to stand up and act with and for. We need to be guided, taught, supported, challenged, and welcomed into whatever arena we might feel compelled to support, and those we might resist supporting. We welcome and need the support and voices of women and persons of color and persons of all sexual identities if we're going to get beyond thinking we still control the world, and if our actions are going to be truly beneficial. We're not going to do this on our own. We tried that for too long. It didn't work.

Listen now, white men. Many people who are not us are afraid and may soon have their lives challenged and changed in ways we will never have to face. Listen to the fear out there, and if you know any fear for your own self and family, listen to how great it is for others. Let it pierce your heart and move you to be a great man of compassion and action.

So white men of courage, selflessness, and generous souls, we invite you to join us as part of the Benevolent Association of White Men Standing Up for Others. We invite women and persons of color to encourage, guide, support, challenge, and welcome us into your struggles. We invite all persons of religions different from our own to tell us how we can stand up for and with you.

What will we do? First, we will make it known that we stand up for others and not for ourselves only. We will not stand for the harmful words and actions of other white men towards others who are different. We will visibly and openly reject racism, sexism, xenophobia, and whatever other-isms separate us from others. We will stand with those who ask for our accompaniment in their struggles for liberation. We will work for a world that is more inclusive and just than the old white man's world ever was.

We can either wallow in fear and grief over losing a world we thought was good, but wasn't, not even for us. Or, we can work hard for the world that is coming, a world where all others with us can live lives of freedom, equity, peace, and well-being.

Join us. Now is the time. Too much is at stake. Stand up for others and be part of the healing balm for our hurting world. Be the man that whiteness never allowed you to be.

+++

What can I say. . . I was motivated and energized and fearful of where our country was going. But, knowing my idea was big and crazy, I decided to share it with some friends, male and female, white and black and Hispanic, and get feedback. The responses were mixed. Some were very positive and encouraged me to go for it. Others were hesitant to provide one more avenue for white men to have a voice when they probably need to listen more. I knew I was not content to do nothing, but what then?

Two months later, the day after the presidential inauguration, the Women's March happened. It was joyful and empowering. It was positive and hopeful. It was determined and unyielding to the messages of those in power. And I felt relief as a man to be participating in something that was motivated, promoted, engineered, and led by women. I could follow and be part of the solution, and not just try to lead all the time.

What does the white church do when it is largely responsible for electing a president feared and resented by much of the non-white church and world? We probably need to let go of trying to be in control and lead everything, which we are used to. Doing nothing is not the right response, but doing something together with others—women, Muslims, African Americans, Hispanics, LGBTQ persons—must be close to a faithful response.

Hey white church. The time has come. The old days are gone when we held the power, and had privilege and priority, and set the norms for what it means to be a Christian and a citizen. We still have a lot of the power, but now we are finding new freedom to let it go. As faithful followers of Jesus (instead of faithful followers of whiteness), we can follow in the way of our fellow African-American, Hispanic, Indigenous, and other non-white churches. We can follow in the way of the cross again, walk in solidarity with all who suffer and are marginalized, and find Jesus again, not in our power and privilege, but in our common need for healing and love.

I had my sense that the white church had a lot more work to do after our annual synod assembly, an annual regional gathering in the Evangelical Lutheran Church of America of leaders and lay persons chosen to be voting members for the assembly. We gather to worship, make decisions both perfunctory and profound, and build relationships across our expansive geographical synod.

At this year's assembly, the opening worship did not set the tone of an inclusive, welcoming gathering. It focused on the German heritage of the Lutheran immigrants who came here in the 19th century. It made use of a "Thanksgiving for Our Heritage" at the opening that quickly said: "us" is white, German Lutheranism. "Them" is those who came after. I do not think this was the intention of the writer or planners. But in a public liturgy, intention is not very important. The impression and the impact is what matters. While other parts of the assembly spoke to a more inclusive, less white-centric church, the opening set a tone that was hard to overcome.

I read this liturgy ahead of time and was surprised and offended. I chose not to attend the worship service so I would not be seen as supporting this exclusive message, and to show solidarity with those who felt left out. One particularly egregious problem with this opening liturgy was the lack of mention of the very old Latino Lutheran congregations in the Rio Grande Valley, some of which are older than most of our majority white congregations. The worship gave the impression that German Lutherans have carried the tradition and then, when the Spirit decided it was time, they recently began to expand their vision to include others through the benevolence of whites.

I'm not looking to blame any particular individuals for this. I am curious how this came to be. All I can guess is that the planning team was not diverse enough to include persons with eyes and ears that would hear this liturgy from a different perspective than the historical, narrow, white experience.

We live with a problem in the Lutheran church, and in other historically white majority denominations, I suspect, one that has been discussed for decades, but with slow progress. We continue to think of the church from a white "us" perspective, and we continue to see the non-white parts of the church as "them," as some other that we benevolently choose to accept among us. We continue to privilege white culture in our decisions and evaluations about worship and church life, rarely even aware that we are doing this, and insensitive to how it continues to exclude and diminish the rich church traditions of many cultures.

It is time to deprivilege the white church. White folks must do it, but we can't do it alone, because we would likely not get it. We should deprivilege the white church in conversation with and relationship with all the parts of the church that comprise the body of Christ. We must lose the sense that we, the white folks, are "us." We need to experience being one part of the body among many, neither privileged, nor rejected, just a part of the wonderful body that only has life when all its parts are honored.

How might we do this? I have a few ideas, but they are only mine and many others have excellent ideas:

1. White folks need to be intentional about deprivileging their own culture in worship. That doesn't mean white culture is bad or should go away. It means opening up to the gifts that other cultures bring and understanding that we have much to learn from them. It means not evaluating everything through the lens of whiteness, but through the lens of the Gospel. Perhaps a majority white congregation or synod should at a minimum always worship with at least one piece of music that isn't Euro-American white, one text that isn't English, one visual that is from cultures of color. While some might criticize this as some form of cultural appropriation, I often hear from non-English speaking persons, or persons of color, who attend such a worship liturgy in a majority white church that they felt more welcomed because of these efforts.

2. Planning for worship and other church events, especially at the regional level, should never be a whites-only group. White people are often not aware of the ways language, liturgy, and music can unintentionally exclude. Even well intended white people who are striving for inclusivity mess this up. White people trying to be inclusive just becomes another exclusive way of doing things.

3. Avoid as much as possible any expression of the church that appears to tell a story that whites were first, and non-whites came later after we decided to let them in. It's a false, white-centered story that often serves merely to make whites feel better about centuries of racist exclusion, and does not speak the truth. It also perpetuates the notion that non-white groups are never the norm, never the center, always defined by how whites decided to accept them. With this, we must find more honest and honorable ways to tell the Native American story even when it disrupts the comfortable white myth of this land and of the church's mission.

4. Practice unending and non-defensive repentance when it comes to being the privileged, white majority. The church lives with the gift of forgiveness and mercy. Use them extravagantly so that we can be open to God's transforming Spirit.

5. White liberals need to be careful about two things: Assuming we have all the right answers to these issues, and being self-righteous in judging other whites when they make mistakes. White conservatives need to be careful about two things: Assuming that admitting to white privilege somehow means losing something, and labeling issues of inclusivity as being only part of the liberal agenda, and not part of the Gospel message itself.

6. Be bold in pursuing justice together in the church and outside the church, and let every worship service and church gathering witness to this. Don't let the fear of making mistakes stop you.

7. Do not begrudge the loss of privilege. Rejoice in the ongoing work of the Spirit to overcome division and create unity within diversity, reconciliation out of division. If that requires letting go of a lot we white folks assumed was a given, then let it go freely and joyfully.

Are We to Wait for Another?

Blessed Is Anyone Who Takes No Offense

Written between the election and the inauguration

At many moments in history, especially times of great uncertainty, it is tempting to look for someone who can bring some sense of safety and security, someone who can fix the mess. During the past eight years beginning with the Great Recession of 2008, but also before that as the Rust Belt grew and globalization left families barely treading water in its wake, many people have struggled. Recovery has come slowly and not reached everyone. The imbalance in the economy before the housing and banking collapse only got worse after that calamity. People need help. Who are they to turn to when it seems like the government, business, and social supports have failed?

Many, it seems, have responded positively to the empty promises of candidate and now president-elect Donald Trump. He came on strong. He promised to fix it (and he alone could do it, he claimed). He gave vast, sweeping sentiment that reached people's hearts and touched their hopes, but provided little actual policy proposals to do anything to help them. And it worked. Or, it worked enough to get him the electoral win, even with a significant popular vote loss. Many people are desperate, or feel that the nation is falling apart, or believe some other kind of irrational but deeply-felt crisis. As has happened before in history, times of economic and social uncertainty create an opportunity for a charismatic and dominating leader to arise.

In the Gospel of Matthew, we hear about a moment in the life of John, the great, late prophet and baptizer. He had been rallying people to prepare the way for the promised one who was coming, the one who would inaugurate God's reign on earth in its fullness, the one who would bring justice and peace and healing to our troubled lives and world. And he said something implausible: he was coming soon! People responded. They repented, were baptized, prepared themselves internally and externally for the one who was to come and was here.

And then Jesus appeared. The beginning of good things unfolded and a new day appeared. Many who had been left behind, left out, and let down saw in Jesus something they had never seen before, or ever even dared hope for: the least were being lifted up first. The good news of Jesus really was good news for all because it started with those who never got good news trickled down on them. This good news would have to trickle up. It was unfolding like a slowly unwrapped gift, and at times it seemed too slow. It was all too good to be true.

Then, John was arrested and waited in prison for his own uncertain future and for greater assurance that Jesus was the one. Could it really be Jesus? He wasn't nearly as irascible and wild as John. He didn't snap his fingers and fix the world. He slowly began to tilt the world in the direction of God's reign of justice, love, and mercy. Like any spinning object with inertia, the world resisted the tilt and pushed back. Still, it was happening. But for John, time was running out and apparently even he didn't expect an anointed leader to rule by pushing up from the bottom of human misery until all were lifted up. Even John couldn't believe the kingdom would come by starting with the stuck, the sick, and the sinner. Even John grew impatient with the pace of God's kingdom.

So John sends a message to Jesus: Are you really him? Are you really the one? Or, should we wait for another? Should we look for a strong man who can fix it all? Should we trust in the dominance of human power to make our lives good again? Or should we trust in your strange ways of love and service and accompaniment with the suffering?

And Jesus says it: Look at what is happening. It's just like Isaiah said. The blind have sight. The deaf can hear. The dead are raised. The poor have good news. Without saying yes, Jesus says yes. God has always been about mercy for the least among us so that they can have life fully, and the most among us can learn mercy and also live life fully. And then Jesus says: Blessed is anyone who takes no offense at me. In other words, blessed is anyone who sees that how I bring about the kingdom, through the least the lost and the lonely, really is the way. You don't have to look for another, Jesus is saying, I am he. You just have to know how to look for the reign of God: at the bottom of the human social order, in acts of compassion, in the powerlessness of love.

For people of faith in Jesus as the One, it is often tempting to look for another. Especially when we are living in painful and unstable social and personal moments, it is highly appealing when someone else can say to us: It's OK, I can fix it, just give me the power. Human history tells us these people often have motives other than benevolent ones. For the body of Christ, faith in Jesus as the way can never be pushed aside for faith in some other way, some other leader, no matter how desperate times are, no matter our own suffering, no matter our inability to believe there is no other other than Jesus.

So the church carries on while the world searches and opines for another. The church gathers in the presence of Christ and sees healing, justice, and mercy come alive. The church practices patience in a world rushing toward uncertain ends. The church lives the kingdom through acts of love that lift up the lowliest among us first, which always lifts up all in the great movement of God's love.

Empires Need Crosses

Sermon for Good Friday

It's an odd thing to say, but we do say it: The cross was necessary. The cross was somehow necessary for something new to happen. Except, don't mistake it: It wasn't necessary for God. God's mercy and life-giving power don't depend on some contrived system of offense and retaliation, or dishonor and required payment, or guilt and sin offering, or anger and appeasement. God is not bound by human notions of fairness or requirements or economic transactions or emotion.

The cross was necessary, but it wasn't necessary for God. That may sound shocking to Christian ears if we bring the baggage of some of the ways God and Jesus and the cross are talked about. But you see, the cross wasn't necessary for God, it was necessary for the Roman empire and for religious power brokers who wanted to be in control of God and people and keep their little safe, secure world unchanged.

It was necessary because right in the midst of Roman rule and religious manipulation of souls came Jesus, the man of peace; Jesus, the man of forgiveness; Jesus, the man for the poor; Jesus, the man of God; Jesus, the man of love; Jesus, the man of healing; Jesus, the man of resistance; Jesus, the man of liberation. And whenever such freedom in God bumps up against the bondage of empires and religions, the cross becomes necessary. And someone must bear it.

In John's Gospel, we get strange language about Jesus and the cross like glorification, Jesus lifted up on the cross for all to see and have eternal life, the lamb of God, the truth, a shining light in the darkness. John's unique Gospel tells us that Jesus was lifted up on the cross to glorify God in himself, to show everyone the truth about empires and religions and all who cower in the darkness, clinging to themselves at all cost, afraid of the liberating light of God's love. So Jesus, the man of love, life, loyalty, and liberation, is lifted up so the cross could expose the Roman empire for what it truly was, expose religious systems of power and control for what they truly are, expose human fear and grasping at straws for what they are: it is all death-dealing instead of life-giving.

In their very game of power and domination Rome and the political, economic, and religious power brokers are exposed for what they are: a lie, a failure, a deathly force. And so is every human system and belief today that seeks the same lies and opposes God. The necessary cross is the truest thing about them so they are exposed, and any part of us that thinks that is the way to construct and live in the world is exposed, too, as hard as that is, and we are changed.

Whenever we gather before the cross, it is all exposed again so that we can be changed again. During the same time of year as Good Friday, Jewish brothers and sister celebrate Passover, the beautiful and sacred ritual that connects Jews to the central story of Jewish faith: liberation. Through a meal shared, a story told, a family gathered at table, and a worldwide but small community joined in prayer, the Passover reminds Jews that they were once a people in bondage, that they were once under oppression, that they were once sure that the Egyptian empire was the way the world was constructed, and that's the way it would always be.

But God liberated them from Egypt to be a people who see the world for what it is: One series of powerful empires after another. God liberated them from Pharaoh's oppression. And God liberated them from their own belief in Pharaoh's destructive power and their doubt about God's merciful, creative power. The Lord God had the Hebrew slaves slaughter a lamb, brush the blood all around their doors, and then eat, huddled together, and celebrate the power of God to liberate. If anyone got scared that Pharaoh might win, they just looked at the blood on the doorway, and they remembered that God was their protection.

When Jesus is crucified in John's Gospel, he is crucified at the moment when the Passover lambs are slaughtered to celebrate God's liberation. In fact, John's timetable is completely different from Matthew, Mark, and Luke, just so he can make this point. John's message is clear even if it is coded in symbolism: Jesus' death is Passover. Jesus' death exposes empire and religion for all their oppressive, deadly forces. Jesus' entire life and death renounce the forces that oppose God, even as he invites the perpetrators of those forces into God's mercy. Jesus' death liberates those who see God in it, who see the truth about this world of selfishness and power grabbing and what it does when we think it is just the way the world is. Jesus' death is necessary for Rome and all empires and religions who oppose God's liberating power. Jesus' death exposes all of our false beliefs and misplaced trust instead of trusting and believing in the God of infinite love, endless mercy, passionate justice, and uncontrollable grace.

How are we to respond to the cross of Jesus, the exposing and liberating cross of Jesus?

I don't think we should respond with guilt. Guilt just makes us think the cross was necessary for God because we are terrible people, and it pushes us away from God. It doesn't draw us toward God, which is the whole point. And then we end up with all the same oppressive religious claims that keep us trapped, not liberated by God.

Imagine you are trapped in a burning building. There's no way for you to get out on your own. And just when you have given up, a fire fighter bursts through the door, takes you to the window, gets you on a ladder, and sends you off to safety. But then, the building is consumed and the fire fighter perishes. Do you look on at the burning timbers with guilt? No, you look on with a deep sense of honor for the life that was given to set you free.

I think our primary response to the cross of Jesus, especially on this Holy Friday, is honor. We honor Jesus for incarnating the love of God so thoroughly and so profoundly, and so courageously and so transformationally, that it necessarily cost him his life. That's what happens in this human world of fearful, unliberated, deathly, power-grabbing sinfulness.

Jesus exposed for us and all the world the ways we lose sight of God and grab hold of the fear-based, blaming, self-preserving, greedy, self-righteous ways of living. And in doing so, he liberates us from all those things and from ourselves. He liberates us for God and for love of neighbor.

Liberation is not an easy thing. It means living and loving freely. It means trusting God more than anything else. It means loving the very persons who persist in what must be renounced. It means seeing the cross as necessary in this world of un-neighborliness, and you might have to bear it in ways you never dreamed of. We honor Jesus by seeing in his cross the exposure of all the false ways, by renouncing all that made the cross necessary, by welcoming and living the liberation it brings, by following him where ever his liberating love leads us, and by standing in silent awe at what God has done for us, and not only us, but all the world, so all may know the liberating power of God's love.

Part Two

RESIST

But Daniel resolved that he would not defile himself with the royal rations of food and wine; so he asked the palace master to allow him not to defile himself. Now God allowed Daniel to receive favor and compassion from the palace master. The palace master said to Daniel, "I am afraid of my lord the king; he has appointed your food and your drink. If he should see you in poorer condition than the other young men of your own age, you would endanger my head with the king." Then Daniel asked the guard whom the palace master had appointed over Daniel, Hananiah, Mishael, and Azariah: "Please test your servants for ten days. Let us be given vegetables to eat and water to drink. You can then compare our appearance with the appearance of the young men who eat the royal rations, and deal with your servants according to what you observe." So he agreed to this proposal and tested them for ten days. At the end of ten days it was observed that they appeared better and fatter than all the young men who had been eating the royal rations. (Daniel 1:8–15)

Humble yourselves therefore under the mighty hand of God, so that he may exalt you in due time. Cast all your anxiety on him, because he cares for you. Discipline yourselves, keep alert. Like a roaring lion your adversary the devil prowls around, looking for someone to devour. Resist him, steadfast in your faith, for you know that your brothers and sisters in all the world are undergoing the same kinds of suffering. And after you have suffered for a little while, the God of all grace, who has called you to his eternal glory in Christ, will himself restore, support, strengthen, and establish you. To him be the power forever and ever. Amen. (1 Peter 5:6–11)

Radical Resistance

Sermon for Epiphany 7 A

The Lord spoke to Moses, saying: Speak to all the congregation of the people of Israel and say to them: You shall be holy, for I the Lord your God am holy. When you reap the harvest of your land, you shall not reap to the very edges of your field, or gather the gleanings of your harvest. You shall not strip your vineyard bare, or gather the fallen grapes of your vineyard; you shall leave them for the poor and the alien: I am the Lord your God. You shall not steal; you shall not deal falsely; and you shall not lie to one another. And you shall not swear falsely by my name, profaning the name of your God: I am the Lord. You shall not defraud your neighbor; you shall not steal; and you shall not keep for yourself the wages of a laborer until morning. You shall not revile the deaf or put a stumbling block before the blind; you shall fear your God: I am the Lord. You shall not render an unjust judgment; you shall not be partial to the poor or defer to the great: with justice you shall judge your neighbor. You shall not go around as a slanderer among your people, and you shall not profit by the blood of your neighbor:

I am the Lord. You shall not hate in your heart anyone of your kin; you shall reprove your neighbor, or you will incur guilt yourself. You shall not take vengeance or bear a grudge against any of your people, but you shall love your neighbor as yourself: I am the Lord. (Leviticus 19:1–2,9–18)

> You have heard that it was said, 'An eye for an eye and a tooth for a tooth.' But I say to you, Do not resist an evildoer. But if anyone strikes you on the right cheek, turn the other also; and if anyone wants to sue you and take your coat, give your cloak as well; and if anyone forces you to go one mile, go also the second mile. Give to everyone who begs from you, and do not refuse anyone who wants to borrow from you. You have heard that it was said, 'You shall love your neighbor and hate your enemy.' But I say to you, Love your enemies and pray for those who persecute you, so that you may be children of your Father in heaven; for he makes his sun rise on the evil and on the good, and sends rain on the righteous and on the unrighteous. For if you love those who love you, what reward do you have? Do not even the tax collectors do the same? And if you greet only your brothers and sisters, what more are you doing than others? Do not even the Gentiles do the same? Be perfect, therefore, as your heavenly Father is perfect. (Matthew 5:38–48)

Hello, holy and perfect people. What? You're not feeling it? Are you worried you might not live up to it? Maybe you're too aware of your faults and failings? Are you feeling down because you tried being perfect, and you went for holy, and it all fell apart, so you gave it up?

Well, Leviticus and Matthew aren't going to let it go. Be holy as God is holy. Be perfect as God is perfect. That's what the texts say. What do you say?

We get some more details in Leviticus and from Jesus. Being holy and perfect like God is holy and perfect looks like this: Don't harvest every stalk of grain and every grape in the vineyard. Leave some around the edges of your property so that when immigrants and the poor travel by they get something to eat, too. Don't revile people with disabilities and make life hard for them; make life good for them. Don't judge people based on whether they are part of your favorite group; judge everyone fairly. Love your neighbor as you love your very self. Don't seek revenge; instead, love your enemy. If you only love those who love you, what's so special about that? Be holy and perfect like God, and love everyone, even your enemy.

Well, those are some of the details. What do you think? How do you rank on the holiness scale? What's your perfection score? When I was a kid I played that game, *Perfection*. There was a board with a bunch of holes in different shapes, and matching pieces for each hole. You had about a minute to put all the pieces in the holes perfectly, and then turn off the timer. Otherwise, the whole board went **pop** and all the pieces flew out. Your perfection score was zero. That's kind of how I feel when I hear Jesus say: *Be perfect.* How is yours? OK, probably not as bad as mine, but still, probably not as good as you think it should be. So what are we to do?

First, if you're one of those perfectionist types, you're going to have to figure out how to let that go. I know it's hard. I know you think you can be perfect if you just try harder. I know you think other people and maybe even God love you because you're pretty darn close to perfect and you can hide all those little flaws and errors. But, come on. It doesn't work. It leads to despair. You're going to have to give that up, and you don't have to give it up perfectly, either.

So what do we do with these calls to holiness and being perfect? Well, we have to stop reading these texts backwards. We should stop reading our lives backwards. We tend to read these texts as if they say: God is holy, so act right and you will be, too. Or, God is perfect, so stop messing up and you will be, too. But in Leviticus, something else is going on. God has already chosen Israel as God's people. God has already liberated and loved them. God has revealed the deep mystery of who God is to them. And because of that, because they are already living in the mystery of God's love, they can be holy as God is holy. Because what makes God holy, what makes God uniquely different, is God's compassion and mercy which Israel already knows in its own life and faith.

And with Jesus, it's the same thing. Jesus has already chosen his disciples. He has already shown them great mercy and compassion. He has already told them they are blessed. He has shown them that God's love is not fickle and easily turned off by messing up. He has shown them how God is perfect, because perfect here means true, single-minded, focused on what really matters all the time, which is living out of love for all, all the time. The disciples know God's love is for all because it is already for them, so to go and be perfect like God is perfect is to go love as you are already loved.

Both Jesus and Leviticus call God's people to live with a generous spirit toward everyone, especially the poor and vulnerable, and yes, even the enemy. Live with a generous spirit toward everyone because this is how God is toward everyone, including you and me. This is how God is holy. This is how God is perfect and true.

It's clear in both texts that God's people are called to be something different from what everyone else thinks is normal. This feels very relevant and urgent in our own time, when the norm seems to be about hating your neighbor and judging people according to your own biases. Be different from the common ways around you! Be different now more than ever! But don't be different in a way that separates you from others. Be different in a way that connects you to others, because that is the very difference we are called to be and live: Connection to everyone and all creation.

These texts show us three important ways to be holy, perfect, different in the way God is those things. First, they speak of living with uncommon generosity. Jesus speaks of giving to those who ask of you. Leviticus commands leaving the edges of the fields and the vineyards unharvested so that wayfarers, immigrants, and the poor can have something to eat. In our culture of maximizing profit and property rights as the absolute good, these texts speak of a different way to be in the world. There's plenty for you, so leave some for others. Be generous, which may be uncommon in a world of selfish greed, but do it even more because it is uncommon.

Second, the texts speak of breaking cycles of hate and violence, and invigorating new cycles of forgiveness and love. Our society often runs in cycles that go unchecked, unexamined, and uninterrupted. Much like cycles of child abuse and neglect, where seventy-five percent of parents involved in child protective services were themselves abused and neglected, our social cycles of hate and violence must be broken for new ways to emerge.

Jesus teaches challenging ways to do this. He teaches not just love of friends and family. He teaches not just doing good to those who do good to you. Those are common and expected practices. They are fine, but they do not break the cycles that take us spiraling downward. Jesus teaches love of enemy. Jesus teaches forgiveness and love of those who persecute you. He teaches showering everyone with love as God showers all with rain (and love). Why? Because showering the enemy with love will transform everything. This is not naïve, passive love that allows the enemy to continue to abuse or oppress you. It is love that exposes the enemy to the hard truth so it can be confronted with you.

Jesus teaches turning the other cheek. This is often quoted and parodied as a kind of submissive posture to the one who strikes. But the implication seems much more daring and challenging: *You can strike me, but you can't take away my dignity and self-respect. Here, I'll show you. Try it again.* Jesus teaches that when a Roman soldier conscripts you to carry his bags a mile (which they could do), go ahead and go two miles. Why? To show that they do not control you. And, because by the time you go the extra mile, the surprised solider may ask you why, and learn that you are guided by a God of uncommon love, and the solider might be changed. This is an act of power, albeit the power of God as embodied in Jesus and known in the cross.

The PBS documentary series *Independent Lens* has an episode called *Accidental Courtesy.* It is about Daryl Davis, a musician who has played keyboard for decades with many well-known musicians in styles from blues and R & B to country. Daryl is African-American and has spent many years doing something somewhat shocking. He has spent a great deal of time and effort befriending members of the Ku Klux Klan. For many of the Klan members, Daryl is the first Black man they have ever gotten to know personally. Daryl does this with a genuine heart. He takes time to learn about the Klan members, some of whom are high up in the organization's hierarchy. He attends meetings. He eats with them. He learns about who they are and shares who he is.

Many Klan members must find this behavior odd and unacceptable. Many who work to expose hate groups and racism may find Daryl's tactics questionable. But Daryl has a closet in his home filled with dozens of clan uniforms, hoods and capes and all. Why? Because his befriending of these enemies has led many to leave their life of hatred and white supremacy behind. They give Daryl their old Klan uniforms as a sign of their leaving, and as a tangible sign of his work, Daryl keeps the uniforms, signs of hate turned into signs of transformation.

Many are talking today, especially in the early days of the Trump presidency, of resisting. Resisting is important in the many forms it is practiced. But resistance is not enough. Only *radical resistance* as Jesus teaches and lived it will transform the world. Only loving your enemies in ways that changes them will work. Love your enemies until they are no longer your enemies is the hard way of Jesus. It is radical resistance that few have dared try, but when they do, enemies become friends.

Jesus is teaching all about following him, about discipleship. Discipleship is about participating in the life of Jesus as God's transforming work in the world, a transformation wrought in acts of love no matter the cost, a transformation unwilling to bend to the ways of hatred and violence to achieve the goals of the kingdom, because what are the goals of the kingdom if not a world without hatred and violence, a world of love and justice and mercy.

God calls us to live fully in God's mercy and love and live fully for God's justice and peace. We are reminded again that we live in a relationship started, nourished, and perfected by God for us.

Know the mystery of Christ living through you, and not just you, but us, this vast body of baptized and Spirit-led people. You didn't do it, you didn't earn it, you didn't even ask for it probably, you're not even sure if you want it all the time. But here you are, here we are, in this particular place and moment of history, somehow knowing it to be the truth, somehow experiencing it in word and sacrament and daily acts of love.

We might be tempted to despair and think: If only the world were more loving and generous and merciful like Jesus. But here's the thing: We are the "if only." We can't wait for everyone else to be lovable. We are God's love loving them into love. And that is perfect. And that is holy.

Xenophilia

It's a Thing and a Christian Virtue

We are living in a time when xenophobia, fear of the other or stranger, is gripping some. It is being used to motivate policies and actions by the government against Muslims, Mexicans and other Latino immigrants, and anyone who some might feel are a threat. It is stirring up hate groups to act out more than they have in recent times. Xenophobia might be the root cause of racism, Islamophobia, homophobia, and other human proclivities to mistrust those outside of our own tribe.

Xenophobia is dangerous. In mild forms, it might keep us in our enclaves, clubs, churches, and segregated neighborhoods, never venturing out to get to know those who are different from us. Unchecked and empowered, it has led to great atrocities in human history, such as the persecution of Jews and the internment of Japanese Americans during World War II.

Many have become familiar with the word xenophobia, especially in our current political climate where so much rhetoric expresses hatred of others. But not many are as familiar with the word xenophilia: Love of the stranger or the other. We don't use it much. It isn't a popular concept for garnering political support. But it is a significant word in the New Testament, even though it only occurs a few times. Consider these verses:

> Contribute to the needs of the saints; extend hospitality to strangers. (Romans 12:13)

> Do not neglect to show hospitality to strangers, for by doing that some have entertained angels without knowing it. (Hebrews 13:2)

In both New Testament letters, showing hospitality to strangers is encouraged as a virtue, the thing that Christians do, and as we read in Hebrews, even a mysterious means of divine communication ("entertaining angels"). But here's the part we miss with our translations: There is no other kind of hospitality other than the kind shown to strangers! The translation turns one word into three.

The word for "hospitality" in both these verses, is, yes, xenophilia (in a slightly different Greek form). Hospitality is not a nice thing we do, serving coffee and donuts after worship, and then we do it better by including strangers. Hospitality simply is loving strangers. Loving the other.

If you're sharing coffee and donuts, or dinner, or throwing a great party, and inviting friends, family, and familiar neighbors, great! It's fun. It's a good thing. It builds up community and family connections. But it isn't hospitality, not in the New Testament sense. We only show hospitality worthy of Christ when we love strangers. Hospitality is xenophilia, and xenophilia is hospitality.

The New Testament encourages hospitality, xenophilia, love of stranger, as a Christian virtue. It is an important part of how the church shows forth the love of God in Christ's name. And if we dig a little deeper, we see that without loving the stranger, we have missed the mark completely.

In Matthew 25, Jesus tells a parable about judgment. It's beautiful and difficult. It's about sheep and goats being separated based on how well they welcomed Christ into their lives. You probably know it. Here is part of it (Matthew 25:35–40):

> I was hungry and you gave me food,
> I was thirsty and you gave me something to drink,
> I was a stranger and you welcomed me,
> I was naked and you gave me clothing,
> I was sick and you took care of me,
> I was in prison and you visited me.'

Then the righteous will answer him,

> 'Lord, when was it that we saw you hungry and gave you food,
> or thirsty and gave you something to drink?
> And when was it that we saw you a stranger and welcomed you,
> or naked and gave you clothing?
> And when was it that we saw you sick or in prison and visited you?'

And the king will answer them,

> 'Truly I tell you, just as you did it
> to one of the least of these who are members of my family,
> you did it to me.'

You see it, of course. *I was a stranger and you welcomed me.* You showed hospitality. You lived xenophilia. You rose above your fear of strangers and lived in utter faith that God has created us to be one in love, and then you did it. And it matters deeply.

Xenophilia is not about how we feel about others, though it might lead to deep feelings of compassion and affection for others. It is about how we love strangers in concrete actions:

- Inviting them into your homes and churches for meals and conversations
- Greeting them on the street with openness and affirmation
- Tipping them well in restaurants and offering words of encouragement for their work
- Standing up for them when others are living out their xenophobia through hateful actions and words
- Listening to their stories of pain and rejection and believing them
- Resisting governmental policies that persecute the "other" for the problems we face in society
- Denying that there is anyone who really is "other" because of our faith in God and the expansive love of Jesus

How else can we live out hospitality, love of the stranger, xenophilia? That's up to us to figure out together as each day comes. We are living in a moment in history when it matters greatly how we do this as a church. We know it matters to Jesus how we love the other. It now matters to us more than ever. And if Hebrews is right, God might be waiting to speak to us some new, wonderful message we will only hear when we welcome and love the stranger.

Peace and love to you, familiars and strangers alike.

Keep Alert! Stay Awake! There Is No New Normal

Written between the election and the inauguration

In the weeks following the presidential election of 2016, the election of Donald Trump to the most powerful office in the world, something odd and unsettling started to happen. After eighteen months of a campaign that stoked fears of Muslims, Mexicans, and Syrian refugees; after insults and intimations of sexual abuse hurled at women; after demeaning comments made about prisoners of war, soldiers killed in battle and their grieving families; and following a reaction to all of this by the press and the public of protest, outrage, anger, and fear. . . unbelievably, it all started to be forgotten or ignored. The most petulant and demagogic presidential candidate in modern American politics won, and so people began to accept it all as some new normal for American life.

This is a frightful loss of a moral conscience in our society. It would be one thing to overlook the immature, hateful, and jingoistic statements of a television celebrity who magnified his ego and popularity via a reality television show. He could carry on publicly damaged, perhaps as some diminished, B-list celebrity showing up on Dancing with the Stars, or as a Comedy Central roast insult comic. We could live with it. We could live with it because we could ignore it with little consequence. But this is the president-elect of the United States of America, the man about to assume an office with great power, influence, and import. To let go of all the words, threats, insults, and frightening policy promises all in the name of acceptance of an election, all because he won, is to lose all claim to being a society of any kind of goodness or righteousness.

In the thirteenth chapter of the Gospel of Mark, we hear what is often called a "little apocalypse." It's a stirring text calling the readers of Mark to faithfulness in a time of fear, in the face of a powerful empire attempting to shape the narrative of their lives. Of course, the narrative they were struggling to live was the story of Jesus, the one sent to bring about God's kingdom of righteousness and justice through humility, powerlessness, and exposure of the empire for all its folly and evil. The power of the Roman empire was great and awful. It was the power to overwhelm one's faith, hope, and memory with a grand, frightful, and strangely alluring hegemony.

I imagine that in the time of Mark's Gospel being written, around 70 AD and the destruction of the Jewish Temple in Jerusalem by the Romans, Jews and Christians were faced with a great temptation: accept this awful reality as the new normal. Give in to the amoral shift happening because it is inevitable and unchangeable. Forget all the great hopes and dreams you had about God shaping a world of love, justice, and mercy. Political, religious, and military power has rendered all that impotent. Take some pills and just let it be.

In that kind of setting, Jesus says in Mark's Gospel:

> But about that day or hour no one knows, neither the angels in heaven, nor the Son, but only the Father. Beware, keep alert; for you do not know when the time will come. It is like a man going on a journey, when he leaves home and puts his servants in charge, each with his work, and commands the doorkeeper to be on the watch. Therefore, keep awake—for you do not know when the master of the house will come, in the evening, or at midnight, or at cockcrow, or at dawn, or else he may find you asleep when he comes suddenly. And what I say to you I say to all: Keep awake. (Mark 13:32–37)

In the face of great and dreadful power, Jesus-followers were called to persistence and resistance. They were called to *beware, keep alert, stay awake.* Those warnings and encouragements are all about not remaking what was happening into a new normal, not accepting what was happening but working against it and working for something far better. And perhaps most important, not letting the ugliness of the empire crush the faith and hope of the people who claim Jesus and his love, his way, his death and resurrection, as the only power and empire that matters.

Nothing could be more relevant in this moment. *Beware! Keep alert! Stay awake! Beware*: the forces of hate that have been stirred up are dangerous and cannot be met with silence. *Keep alert*: the rhetoric of fear mongering is dangerous and must still be resisted. *Stay awake*: it is all too easy to fall asleep now and hope this is all a bad dream. It isn't. It is real. Faith matters now more than ever.

There is no new normal of racism, xenophobia, and misogyny that can be accepted or acquiesced to simply because we have grown tired of resisting it, and the one who spouted it all is now about to become president. There is no new normal just because television news and written journalism have stopped pushing back as hard. There is no new normal for those who live by faith, who are wary, alert, and awake to what is going on. For those who put their faith in God and the kingdom coming through Christ Jesus, there is not a new normal, but a new wonderful. And it is not so far from us, and may be arriving through our witness and our actions of love, justice, and mercy.

Keep alert. Stay awake. Now more than ever.

Fasting for Strength

Resistance as an act of faith, while living in a world drastically opposed to the beliefs and practices of that faith, is hard and wearisome work. There shouldn't be too much romanticizing about what it means to live in resistance to the dominant culture and operative forces that surround us. It is a daily decision for difference. It is an ongoing acceptance of paying a price. It is a lifelong struggle against pure self-interest and pursuit of comfort. No one should take up the mantle of following Jesus innocently or naively. They will quickly and surely be disappointed and not last long in the way of the cross. Jesus himself said:

> Now large crowds were traveling with him; and he turned and said to them, "Whoever comes to me and does not hate father and mother, wife and children, brothers and sisters, yes, and even life itself, cannot be my disciple. Whoever does not carry the cross and follow me cannot be my disciple. For which of you, intending to build a tower, does not first sit down and estimate the cost, to see whether he has enough to complete it? (Luke 14:25–28)

What does Christian resistance look like in times and places where demagoguery is the voice of politics, when playing on people's basest fears and desires is the primary means of gaining support, when the dominant social and political group scrambles to regain power by openly rejecting the dignity and place in society of all those who are thought to be "other?" It must surely look like:

- fasting from the very things the empire offers that entice us to non-resistance
- non-participation in privileged status by those who have such privilege
- open protest and criticism of dangerous leaders and policies, and
- the communal and ritual enactment of a different way of life that by its very visibility critiques the deathly, dominant way.

None of this is easily spelled out in advance how to do it. Resistance that simply mimics past resistance will not have much transforming power. But there are stories and examples from Scripture and history that inspire us to imagine what faithful resistance looks like in our own contemporary struggle. Telling these stories is an essential part of energizing and funding the faithful imagination.

The book of Daniel is a complex and rich resource for stirring a faithful imagination for resistance. It is set in the period of Israel's exile in the sixth century B. C. E., when Babylon wielded fearsome power to crush the nation. It did so through military force, by establishing vassal monarchs, and eventually, exiling many of the people far away to the land of Babylon to live under the rule of King Nebuchadnezzar, exiling especially the powerful, wealthy, and educated. During this time, with Jerusalem in ruins, those who were left lived a difficult and hardscrabble existence. Those who were exiled in Babylon struggled with questions of how to remain faithful in a foreign and hostile land, how much to accommodate to Babylonian ways, and how much to maintain Jewish uniqueness and faith in the God who once said that the kingdom centered in Jerusalem would never end.

Daniel includes numerous apocalyptic visions and stories about the prophet and his friends and how they maintained faithfulness in exile. What makes the book even more compelling for us today is the historical-critical realization that while the book is set in the exile, it was likely composed or redacted in the later period of the Seleucid Empire in the second century B. C. E. when the Maccabees were themselves striving to live out faithful resistance after the Greek empire had trampled their land. The author or authors of Daniel realized that telling the stories of resistance the ancestors had lived would empower the contemporary community to find its way to faithful resistance.

This work was so powerful a witness to resistance that when Mark wrote his Gospel story about Jesus, he incorporated elements of Daniel in the "little apocalypse" of chapter 13. In doing so, Mark reminds his readers during a period of Roman oppression that their ancestors, and their ancestors' ancestors, had resisted their empire's attempts to dominate. Resistance is always fueled by memories of past resistance even when that resistance was costly. Surely an uncountable number of Christian communities have been inspired by the Gospels' witness to Jesus' and the disciples' acts of resistance to the empire, and by telling this story as the good news of God, found their way to faithful resistance in their lives. The impact of reading Scripture in Christian worship on a regular basis, particularly those texts that make explicit resistance to the empire a central theme, have inspiring power for us today.

One story in particular from Daniel that stirs our imaginations for faithful resistance is from chapter one. It begins like this:

> In the third year of the reign of King Jehoiakim of Judah, King Nebuchadnezzar of Babylon came to Jerusalem and besieged it. The Lord let King Jehoiakim of Judah fall into his power, as well as some of the vessels of the house of God. These he brought to the land of Shinar, and placed the vessels in the treasury of his gods. (Daniel 1:1–2)

Jerusalem is besieged and the holy objects from the temple are stolen and placed before Babylonian gods. A Jewish reader starting this story would immediately be offended and stirred up to resistance. But then the next part comes:

> Then the king commanded his palace master Ashpenaz to bring some of the Israelites of the royal family and of the nobility, young men without physical defect and handsome, versed in every branch of wisdom, endowed with knowledge and insight, and competent to serve in

> the king's palace; they were to be taught the literature and language of the Chaldeans. The king assigned them a daily portion of the royal rations of food and wine. They were to be educated for three years, so that at the end of that time they could be stationed in the king's court. Among them were Daniel, Hananiah, Mishael, and Azariah, from the tribe of Judah. The palace master gave them other names: Daniel he called Belteshazzar, Hananiah he called Shadrach, Mishael he called Meshach, and Azariah he called Abednego. (Daniel 1:3–7)

Just after hearing about the horrors of being conquered and having sacred objects profaned, we hear that the king is looking for some Jewish leaders to go along with it all, to accept being conquered and serve the king. They were to be educated (indoctrinated) into the ways of the empire, slowly having their minds and souls shaped to forget who they are as Jews who lived by God's justice, and in that amnesia, live instead by the violent and unjust ways of Nebuchadnezzar. Perhaps most notable, they were to have their names changed from their Jewish identity to new Babylonian names with a new corresponding identity. Any reader in late Judaism hearing this story must wonder: Will Daniel and the rest go along with this, or will they resist?

The answer is complex and invites interpretation for contemporary needs. In some sense, they do go along. They find positions of power within the king's court. They need to survive. At the same time, we hear that they will only go along so much, and will not completely accommodate themselves to the empire. They will confess their faith in the God of Israel, and to help them do that, they will fast:

> But Daniel resolved that he would not defile himself with the royal rations of food and wine; so he asked the palace master to allow him not to defile himself. (Daniel 1:8)

Daniel refuses to eat the royal rations. Royal food is such a rich symbol the reader is left to ponder what exactly might qualify as royal food. What is the empire offering to me as nourishment that tempts me because it taps into my hunger? Whatever that is,

Daniel refuses to consume it. Instead, he and the others only eat "vegetables," the plain and simple food one needs to get by without buying into royal food.

One would expect that such fasting and such meager sustenance would lead one to lose weight, lose strength, grow weary, and perhaps be tempted even more to eat the king's provisions. But the text says what actually happened:

> At the end of ten days it was observed that they appeared better and fatter than all the young men who had been eating the royal rations. So the guard continued to withdraw their royal rations and the wine they were to drink, and gave them vegetables. To these four young men God gave knowledge and skill in every aspect of literature and wisdom; Daniel also had insight into all visions and dreams. (Daniel 1:15–17)

The impression one gets from reading this text is that resistance requires fasting from something, giving something up, not consuming everything the empire has to offer, especially whatever is rich and full of marrow and tempting to the stomach and the soul. And this resistance, this fasting, is true nourishment, true strength for faithful people. It is nourishment and strength because such resistance and fasting is blessed by God, who is the very nourishment and strength any faithful person needs.

The text goes on to narrate how it is Daniel and the others work within the king's court, face other trials and temptations, and maintain faithfulness throughout. More so, the text illustrates that God maintains faithfulness to his people who struggle to resist even as they live in an empire that requires some level of cooperation.

Resistance is not clear-cut. It is not about purity and absolutes. It is about compromises and working within systems even as one seeks to transform them. At the same time, it does require discerning when and how to fast, what to give up, what to reject for one's self for the sake of faithfulness. For those who live by faith, the message is strong and clear: Fasting as resistance may be necessary, but when taken up as one's calling, such fasting strengthens and emboldens. It does not starve and weaken. If God is blessing our resistance, our fasting, our complicated negotiations for and against the vast empires we live under, then we will have all the muscle and energy we need to endure and thrive.

Alternative Facts

The Theology of Glory

1. ALTERNATIVE FACTS

DURING THE EARLY DAYS of the Trump administration, a transparent and shocking moment occurred on live television. It was a moment we rarely see from those wielding unchecked power, because they usually keep truth guarded and occluded. After two days of the White House arguing about the crowd size at the president's inauguration (because, apparently, bigger is always better), Kellyanne Conway, official counselor to the president, appeared on *Meet the Press* to defend Sean Spicer, the White House press secretary. The day before, Spicer had appeared for his first press conference. He was angry, terse, and accusatory toward the press because they had reported, accurately and with photographic evidence, that the crowd in attendance for the presidential inauguration was significantly smaller than Barack Obama's first inauguration in 2009. In a world of facts and mature politics, none of this should matter, but of course, it offended the egos of the President and his aids. Spicer defended the claim that the attendance for Trump's inauguration was the largest ever with a number of statements that were clearly false.

Conway appeared on the Sunday morning political talk shows the next day. Conway excels at political spin and obfuscation, something all political parties and those who win elections do constantly. Conway is perhaps the best spin doctor in modern politics. But she may have met her match in Chuck Todd on *Meet the Press*. Questioning Conway about Spicer's claims regarding attendance numbers, Todd pushed her on Spicer's falsehoods. Then Conway, perhaps in a moment of frustration or weariness, said what may become a defining term for the Trump presidency: Spicer was using "alternative facts." To this, Todd responded with an important moment in truth-telling against the lies of power: *Alternative facts are not facts. They are falsehoods.*

In that moment, Conway embodied and revealed the struggle of those in power who wish to wield power without limits: the truth must be killed in order to do so. From the brilliant and eerily relevant *1984* by George Orwell, to the manipulation of international affairs by William Randolph Hearst through yellow journalism, we have seen throughout history how truth is manipulated for the sake of power. As is often quoted (attributed to Hiram Johnson, U. S. senator from California from 1917 to 1945): *The first casualty, when war comes, is truth.*

In 2006, the Merriam-Webster word of the year was *truthiness.* The word was coined by Stephen Colbert on his Comedy Central program, *The Colbert Report.* On the show, Colbert played a bloviating conservative commentator most often compared to Bill O'Reilly. At the time, Colbert was satirizing the George W. Bush administration's blurring of facts. *Truthiness* means truth not based on facts but on a feeling in the gut, or whatever feels good to the person or suits the political needs of the moment. It is truth that we wish were true, rather than what actually is true. We might be in a new age of *truthiness.*

2. THEOLOGY OF GLORY

The year 2017 marks the 500th anniversary of the Lutheran reformation. On October 31, 1517, Martin Luther posted his 95 Theses, statements challenging current church teaching and practice. While many events led up to and followed this moment that shaped the revolution that was the Reformation, this key event stands out as a tipping point, a moment when Luther questioned what was accepted as truth in his day. It may be unexpectedly important in ways no one could have predicted to mark the 500th anniversary of this history-changing event and reconsider its importance for our own day.

One of the most important contributions from Martin Luther's writings is his understanding of what he called the Theology of Glory. Luther was exploring his hard-wrought theology during a time of highly concentrated power, both in the church and in the empire. He witnessed firsthand how alternative facts came to reign, how truthiness was preferred to truth by those who held power over the people by controlling what counted as facts, truth, and reality. Luther understood with great insight how those in power will use their power for their own sake, and will lie to maintain power.

After Luther posted his 95 Theses in 1517, he was embroiled in controversy and needed to defend his positions. In 1518 at his Augustinian order, the Heidelberg Disputation was held. It is in this work that Luther first articulates his understanding of the Theology of Glory, and its counterpart, the Theology of the Cross. In one of his most pregnant statements, Luther wrote:

> A theology of glory calls evil good and good evil.
> A theology of the cross calls the thing what it actually is.

Luther understood that the political and religious powers were all seeking glory, and claimed God was in the same game. The fundamental theological issue was whether God was found in the halls of power and success and the dishonest mask of human righteousness, or whether God was found among the suffering, sinful, poor, powerless reality that most people knew to be true. In order to maintain a theology of glory, not to mention a politics and ecclesiology of glory that flowed from it, the very evils of the world had to be called good. Concentrated power and wealth that left people suffering poverty and injustice: good! Abuse of position and authority that swept people's lives into a trash heap: good!

Maintenance of a religious system rooted in self-righteousness and earned privilege that made it impossible for real people ever to attain a transformational relationship with God rooted in grace and mercy: good!

The antidote as Luther understood it was to know God through Christ on the cross, to start there and always there and let all other truth flow from the cross. If God is revealed in suffering, then what does that say about all the suffering of the world and those who cause suffering? If God is revealed in powerlessness, then what does that say about the powerless of the world and those who hold power over them? If God is revealed in self-giving love then what does that say about all those who have been indoctrinated with love that must be earned, and those who did the indoctrination? This was not some esoteric theological pondering about atonement theory. This was a deep and concrete pondering of how God is known and for whom God is acting in the world. And the message was startling and clear: God was not held captive to bishops and princes and halls of glory. God was in the world as Christ was on the cross: In suffering and in compassion that pours out to all those in need.

Once Luther dethroned the privilege of glory as it pertained to God's redemptive work, the cross became the powerful way for truth to be told. No suffering can be distorted into something good. No injustice can be turned into an alternative fact of justice. No truthiness that tells the news in a way that feels good to and supports those in power can be allowed to stand as the truth. The truth of human life and injustice and suffering and the evil machinations of human power is an ugly truth exposed on the cross of Christ for all to see and never to be turned into an alternative truth that denies this is how things are. The cross is God's truth so that truth can transform.

3. ROYAL TRUTHINESS OF GLORY

During the reign of King Solomon in ancient Israel, there was a surge of coalescing power, wealth, and control. Solomon seemed to love big, shiny opulence, and brought the nation to ruin in achieving his self-aggrandizing and destructive goals. The Bible remembers this enticing and dangerous path, and narrates it from several perspectives. The beginning of Solomon's reign is narrated simply and positively:

> So Solomon sat on the throne of his father David;
> and his kingdom was firmly established. (1 Kings 2:12)

It sounds solid. Solomon's reign is rooted in the memory of his father David's reign, the great and good king of Israel. Then the claims of this inaugural affirmation are immediately undermined by the first official act of Solomon. Solomon's older brother, Adonijah, sheepishly asks Solomon through Bathsheba, Solomon's mother, for permission to marry Abishag the Shunamite. She reports the request to Solomon, whose immediate reaction is thoughts of conspiracy and fear of losing power, so he has his brother Adonijah killed. The narrative of killing and persecution continues through the end of the chapter.

Reading this chapter, the reader wonders how to interpret the beginning affirmation: *His kingdom was firmly established.* Is this presented as a factual statement, then affirmed by the series of revenge murders and paranoid conspiracy thoughts? Or is this first statement the official alternative fact of the Solomon administration, which is then shown to be false through truth telling and irony? The text may be ambiguous, but its very ambiguity makes a flat, affirmative reading of royal power questionable.

The Solomon narrative continues through the building of the temple and the king's house. It is noteworthy that the king's house ends up being larger and more opulent than the Lord's house, the temple. It is as if the temple was built to make God happy and keep God from noticing how grand and gold the palace was. The temple is a shiny object and an alternative fact meant to distract from the palace.

In order to accomplish these majestic building projects and support his excessive lifestyle, Solomon must heavily tax the people, enslave foreigners in his own land, and create a standing army through conscription. All of this is narrated plainly, with the alternative fact thrown in to mollify and distract from the just stated awful facts:

> But of the Israelites Solomon made no slaves; they were the soldiers, they were his officials, his commanders, his captains, and the commanders of his chariotry and cavalry. (1 Kings 9:22)

Now, one could surmise that all of this is intended to show the glory and blessed character of Solomon's reign, that the Lord is pleased with Solomon's excess and violence. But these verses narrating Solomon's heavy taxation, enslavement, and militarization of Israel immediately bring to mind the beginning of the Samuel and Kings narrative that foreshadowed all of this. The extensive narrative of the period of Israel's kings begins with Samuel arguing with the people because they want a king like other nations have for the sake of security and pride. Samuel tells them no. Samuel reminds them that only the Lord will be their king. The prescient verses in this exchange are:

> So Samuel reported all the words of the Lord to the people who were asking him for a king. He said, "These will be the ways of the king who will reign over you: he will take your sons and appoint them to his chariots and to be his horsemen, and to run before his chariots; and he will appoint for himself commanders of thousands and commanders of fifties, and some to plow his ground and to reap his harvest, and to make his implements of war and the equipment of his chariots. He will take your daughters to be perfumers and cooks and bakers. He will take the best of your fields and vineyards and olive orchards and give them to his courtiers. He will take one-tenth of your grain and of your vineyards and give it to his officers and his courtiers. He will take your male and female slaves, and the best of your cattle and donkeys, and put them to his work. He will take one-tenth of your flocks, and you shall be his slaves. And in that day you will cry out because of your king, whom you have chosen for yourselves; but the Lord will not answer you in

> that day." But the people refused to listen to the voice of Samuel; they said, "No! but we are determined to have a king over us, so that we also may be like other nations, and that our king may govern us and go out before us and fight our battles." (1 Samuel 8:10–20)

The entire story of Israel's first kings begins with a warning, which then plays out over the reign of the first three kings. The narrative follows with the first king, Saul, who after a series of failures is removed from the throne by God's command. Then follows the reign of David, the beloved king who is shown to be faithful to God, while at the same time he is shown to be flawed, selfish, and the initial cause of the rise and fall of Solomon and the kingdom of Israel. And then we get Solomon, who is portrayed as wise and grand, while at the same time shown to be excessive, power hungry, vengeful, and unfaithful to God. Solomon's reign embodies the warnings of the Lord spoken through Samuel to the people at their request for a king. The reign of Solomon ends with this:

> Then the Lord was angry with Solomon, because his heart had turned away from the Lord, the God of Israel, who had appeared to him twice, and had commanded him concerning this matter, that he should not follow other gods; but he did not observe what the Lord commanded. Therefore the Lord said to Solomon, "Since this has been your mind and you have not kept my covenant and my statutes that I have commanded you, I will surely tear the kingdom from you and give it to your servant. Yet for the sake of your father David I will not do it in your lifetime; I will tear it out of the hand of your son. I will not, however, tear away the entire kingdom; I will give one tribe to your son, for the sake of my servant David and for the sake of Jerusalem, which I have chosen." (1 Kings 11:9–13)

Solomon's administration ends with the kingdom divided. The narrative bends the story to make clear that the promise of God to David remains intact, but only in a highly modified and diminished way. In reading this grand arc of a story, how are we to read the accounts of greatness, accomplishment, blessedness, and grandeur that came before? They seem at best a sad irony. They come to us perhaps through an official account of alternative facts, the spin the monarchy put on the story as it was unfolding for the truth not to be seen but kept shrouded in misdirection and fog. However the positive spin on the monarchy comes to us through tradition and redaction, it is clear from the narrative as a whole that the facts of the matter are that unchecked power in the hands of humans ruled by their own egos and self-deception leads away from God's reign, leads to corruption and abuse of people, leads to ruin and destruction for the nation. The theology of glory reigns all too often, and lies must be told to prop it up.

The entire kingly story of Samuel and Kings is a meta-narrative on truth-telling amid alternative facts. It is a strong witness to the one truth that monarchs and presidents never want to hear: the truth will always come through because God is a God of truth. Injustice and oppression always come with some form of lie to sustain them, but the God of truth and justice always brings injustice and oppression to an end and exposes the lies, the alternative facts, the cost to human lives of unchecked greed and power. The theology of glory always gets exposed through the cross for the lie that it is. And then, through the starkness of the truth of human injustice and oppression and sin, new possibilities emerge.

The narrative brings a kind of sustained, if haggard, hope. It does not say that kings and leaders will never arise who abuse their power and their people for their own ends. It does not say that a nation that is obedient to the Lord in appearance will have blessing forever. The narrative does not support the lies of a theology of glory. It shows that the ugly truth of human injustice and distorted power will always be exposed so that God can bring newness. The royal narratives of the Bible always show the end of human folly, but they never stop there. They always go on to show the life-giving power of God beyond the death-dealing powers of people. Hope is always the proper direction to head when one is steered by faith in the God of Scripture, even if the journey is long, injurious, and through seas of fog.

4. THEOLOGY OF THE CROSS IN DEMOCRACY

We do not have kings. We do not have dictators. We do not have endless inheritances of power from one royal family to the next. We have a democracy where power is held by the people, and given to elected leaders as a trust. We have a free press where truth can be told unfettered by those wielding political power. We have freedom of religious practice where truth telling in pulpits and on street corners cannot be crushed. At least, these are our ideals. The practice of them may be much more nuanced, complicated, and complicit with political power and seeking after glory, even and sometimes especially among religions.

We are living in a time when truth itself is being challenged, distorted, and at times, blatantly manipulated. As Daniel Patrick Moynihan once said: *You are entitled to your opinion. You are not entitled to your own facts.* Yet, we are frequently hearing people claiming their own facts when the truth doesn't fit their agenda. A theology of glory is assumed and practiced everywhere, even if the practitioners don't hold an explicit theological framework for it. How is the church to witness and act in such a time when truth itself is apparently up for grabs? A few suggestions:

i. The church always begins by being brutally honest about itself, to itself, before God, and with the world. The errors, misguided efforts, gross sins, and subtly complicit ways of the church with injustice in the world must be confessed and exposed unadorned. This is no time (not that there ever is a time for such a thing) for the church to equivocate, obfuscate, or deny its own striving after glory and power, its own failure to serve and care for those in need, its own abusive and harmful history. The church exists as a community so deeply rooted in God's grace that it need not and boldly rejects telling lies about itself. To do so is to deny and diminish God's grace for its own life and for the world. A community living out of God's infinite mercy never fears the truth, only the lies that hide the truth. The church lives always under the cross.

ii. The church amplifies the voices of truth of people who are oppressed. Standing in solidarity with people in the cross of Christ means helping their voices get heard in the halls of government and justice. Immigrants, refugees, poor minorities, persons with disabilities, and many others are simply not heard by our leaders. Their voices are not powerful enough to break through the loudness of money and mutual favors. The church has the megaphone of the pulpit and the public sphere and despite vast cultural changes regarding religion, the church's voice is still heard. The church has real estate which can display the word in highly visible ways. Clergy still garner some social respect, and must use that respect and whatever other power they have in cultural and political spheres to speak in support of those longing to be heard.

iii. The church supports other truth telling than its own. This may sound strange for a community committed to a peculiar and particular message that is Jesus. But one way the church witnesses to the truth of the good news is to support it whenever it is being enacted elsewhere in the world. The church in true humility knows it does not own the truth even as it claims to be in the truth. God owns the truth and the church dare not limit where and how God will reveal and enact this truth. When Muslims speak the truth about God's justice, the church should give praise. When Jews speak out for the oppressed, the church should shout its approval. When the press and the university and secular institutions and any political party witness to and work for the truth of God's mercy for all people, the church gives its joyful thanks.

iv. The church witnesses to the hope of the Gospel revealed in the strange world of Scripture and in the death and resurrection of Christ: The cries of the poor and oppressed are heard by God and responded to, because even when the recalcitrant powerful have their eyes and ears shut to the truth, God's eyes and ears are open. And because God hears and sees the truth, and is a God of love and mercy, the good news will not be stopped by any human power. Psalm 34 stunningly witnesses to this most important and unstoppable truth:

> Come, O children, listen to me; I will teach you the fear of the Lord.
> Which of you desires life, and covets many days to enjoy good?

Keep your tongue from evil, and your lips from speaking deceit.
Depart from evil, and do good; seek peace, and pursue it.
The eyes of the Lord are on the righteous, and his ears are open
to their cry.
The face of the Lord is against evildoers,
to cut off the remembrance of them from the earth.
When the righteous cry for help, the Lord hears,
and rescues them from all their troubles.
The Lord is near to the brokenhearted, and saves the crushed in
spirit.
Many are the afflictions of the righteous,
but the Lord rescues them from them all.
He keeps all their bones; not one of them will be broken.
Evil brings death to the wicked,
and those who hate the righteous will be condemned.
The Lord redeems the life of his servants;
none of those who take refuge in him will be condemned.
(Psalm 34:11–22)

v. Finally, the church witnesses to the truth by refusing to fall into the lure of despair when times become challenging. The church gathers even in its confusion to celebrate the good news, because it knows the only truth that matters and has sway and endures is the good news of God's love, justice, and mercy unleashed in the world through Jesus Christ. Even as it renounces and resists, the church is always and ever rejoicing.

Part Three

REJOICE

Then the mystery was revealed to Daniel in a vision of the night, and Daniel blessed the God of heaven. Daniel said: "Blessed be the name of God from age to age, for wisdom and power are his. He changes times and seasons, deposes kings and sets up kings; he gives wisdom to the wise and knowledge to those who have understanding. He reveals deep and hidden things; he knows what is in the darkness, and light dwells with him. To you, O God of my ancestors, I give thanks and praise, for you have given me wisdom and power, and have now revealed to me what we asked of you, for you have revealed to us what the king ordered." (Daniel 2:19–23)

Blessed be the God and Father of our Lord Jesus Christ! By his great mercy he has given us a new birth into a living hope through the resurrection of Jesus Christ from the dead, and into an inheritance that is imperishable, undefiled, and unfading, kept in heaven for you, who are being protected by the power of God through faith for a salvation ready to be revealed in the last time. In this you rejoice, even if now for a little while you have had to suffer various trials, so that the genuineness of your faith—being more precious than gold that, though perishable, is tested by fire—may be found to result in praise and glory and honor when Jesus Christ is revealed. Although you have not seen him, you love him; and even though you do not see him now, you believe in him and rejoice with an indescribable and glorious joy, for you are receiving the outcome of your faith, the salvation of your souls. (1 Peter 1:3–9)

Magnificat March

Rejoicing in Lowliness

And Mary said,

"My soul magnifies the Lord,
  and my spirit rejoices in God my Savior,
for he has looked with favor on the lowliness of his servant.
  Surely, from now on all generations will call me blessed;
for the Mighty One has done great things for me,
  and holy is his name.
His mercy is for those who fear him
  from generation to generation.
He has shown strength with his arm;
  he has scattered the proud in the thoughts of their hearts.
He has brought down the powerful from their thrones,
  and lifted up the lowly;
he has filled the hungry with good things,
  and sent the rich away empty.
He has helped his servant Israel,
  in remembrance of his mercy,
according to the promise he made to our ancestors,
  to Abraham and to his descendants forever." (Luke 1:46–55)

JANUARY 21, 2017 WILL be remembered as a day that marked a shift in the political direction of the nation. It was also a day that called many in the church to step out in new ways. The Women's March became the largest demonstration in the history of the United States. Across all fifty states, in large cities and small towns, people came out and said they would not allow the government to demean women and lead the nation backwards when it comes to women's rights.

My wife and I attended the march in Austin, Texas. We arrived at the rugged stone capitol a few minutes before the start time, entered on the west side, and quickly found it so crowded we couldn't make our way to the front. We spent the next hour-and-a-half slowly inching toward the south exit of the grounds onto Congress Avenue where the march itself was taking place. It was hot and we had no water and since we couldn't tell exactly what was going on, it was frustrating to be moving so slowly. But while we were frustrated, we were entertained by the hundreds of creative and pointed-messaged signs. Some of them were verging on offensive, and some of them were inspiring.

A wide array of people was there: men and women, families with kids, Muslims and Christians and Jews, elders and infants. The police were helpful and supportive. The crowd was calm and energized at the same time. Once we made our way out to the march in the streets, people on the sidewalks, on hotel balconies, and on side streets were cheering and showing thumbs up. By the end of the march, it felt like our fragile democracy, which had seemed to be under attack, had strong legs and muscles to keep moving forward.

After the march, this occurred to me: The church is too often a follower and not a leader in speaking and acting publicly on behalf of those who are marginalized and struggling. I wondered what the church could do *as church* in public to witness in a powerful way that, through its message and through its means, would help give voice with and for the voiceless and the seldom listened to.

The idea blossomed into a dream of a Magnificat March. The Magnificat is the song of Mary in the Gospel of Luke. It celebrates that God was acting in bringing to birth the Messiah who would honor and redeem the lowly of the earth. Mary herself experienced profound humility in the announcement of her pregnancy and significance of her child. This deep humble encounter with God is itself a story of the good news: God works through the lowly to accomplish God's will for all the world.

The song itself is a radical, shocking, challenging transformation of the world order wrought by God's iron will. The lowly are lifted up, the powerful are brought down. Those who fear God are shown mercy, the proud are scattered like leaves in a stormy wind. The hungry are fed with good things. The wealthy are sent away hungry. Much like Jesus' blessings in Matthew's and Luke's Gospel, this is a radical re-orientation of who matters and how God transforms the world into a place of mercy, justice, love, and peace. It isn't through the powerful governments and their war machines and their proclivity towards inhumane and unjust means. It isn't through the wealthy and their self-deceiving ways of bending human systems toward their benefit alone. God works through the poor, hungry, lowly, and humble, the same people Jesus associated with and called to be his new community.

What I imagine, then, is the church leading a Magnificat March, a public witness across the nation that lifts up the voices of the lowly, the marginalized, those threatened by the government's shift toward xenophobic policies. Churches in every city could organize a Magnificat March on the same day with the same purpose, organize with and not just for those whose voices are silenced by the political and social forces of domination. One possible unified date for such a march would be the Feast of the Visitation, celebrated in the west on May 31. This is the day to tell the story of Mary's visit with Elizabeth, when Mary sings her world-transforming song.

I garnered some interest in the idea in early 2017 through social networking. However, I am not skilled at organizing such a large event. I share this because I think something like this is how the church could and should live out its faith publicly. Perhaps there are better ways to do it. Maybe it needs to be done in deeper partnership with other groups. Many of course are already marching and magnifying the name of God in their witness to God's compassion for the lowly. Most notable today, the Rev. Dr. William J. Barber, II and the organization he leads, Repairers of the Breach, are marching and echoing the song of Mary in powerful ways. However it happens, the church gathering to march, sing, pray, and speak out a public Magnificat is surely needed in these times.

It also occurred to me that the church in its regular gatherings is always a community of the Magnificat, always a song and a march witnessing to God's kingdom and lifting up those who are trampled down in the city streets and small towns of the world. Every Sunday liturgy and every communion table is the church's chance to march and sing and celebrate and challenge with the good news of God's kingdom. The church is always a good news gathering where the humble are welcomed with the honor usually reserved for kings and queens, the hungry are fed without cost or need to prove one's worth or citizenship, the powerful are welcomed, too, but by the very act of humbly receiving God's grace with everyone else, they are brought down low.

The church's liturgy is always a public and political statement, and never a partisan one. We might need to make that even more obvious in these days when many lowly are still waiting to be lifted up. We may need to rejoice in the Gospel with more exuberance and public witness than we ever have. In doing so, all will be lifted up.

Born of Wind and Water

Sermon for Lent 2 A

The Lord said to Abram, "Go from your country and your kindred and your father's house to the land that I will show you. I will make of you a great nation, and I will bless you, and make your name great, so that you will be a blessing. I will bless those who bless you, and the one who curses you I will curse; and in you all the families of the earth shall be blessed." So Abram went, as the Lord had told him; and Lot went with him. (Genesis 12:1–4a)

Now there was a Pharisee named Nicodemus, a leader of the Jews. He came to Jesus by night and said to him, "Rabbi, we know that you are a teacher who has come from God; for no one can do these signs that you do apart from the presence of God." Jesus answered him, "Very truly, I tell you, no one can see the kingdom of God without being born from above." Nicodemus said to him, "How can anyone be born after having grown old? Can one enter a second time into the mother's womb and be born?" Jesus answered, "Very truly, I tell you, no one can enter the kingdom of God without being born of water and Spirit. What is born of the flesh is flesh, and what is born of the Spirit is spirit. Do not be astonished that I said to you, 'You must be born from above.' The wind blows where it chooses, and you hear the sound of it, but you do not know where it comes from or where it

> goes. So it is with everyone who is born of the Spirit." Nicodemus said to him, "How can these things be?" Jesus answered him, "Are you a teacher of Israel, and yet you do not understand these things? (John 3:1–10)

The church rejoices that it lives a new life in Christ, a life of love for God and others that it did not generate for itself, but experiences as a constantly given gift of God through Christ by the power of the Spirit. This life is not always clear and automatically submitted to. At times, it seems incomprehensible and we resist what we should embrace. How do we live the love of God in an age when that love is rejected? How do we live a new life in an old world?

Jesus and Nicodemus are having a perplexing conversation about eternal life. And before we try to make sense of that, I must ask: Does anyone care about that anymore? The theologian Douglas John Hall once wrote: *People used to ask, "Is there life after death?" Now people are asking, "Is there life before death?"*

When we hear Jesus talk about "eternal life" and how we get it, I'm guessing we assume he is talking about life after death. But in John's Gospel, the phrase "eternal life" has a unique meaning of life before death, life lived in all its fullness, life lived in the love of God here and now. Eternal life in John includes the idea of life after death. But rather than focus on the length of life, it is first about the quality of life, the kind of life we live now. And the question is: Is life as we know it limited and empty of meaning, or is it infinite and full of love.

Nicodemus comes to Jesus because he is curious enough about him. Nick saw Jesus do some great things. Nick said he knows God must be at work in Jesus. But Jesus challenges him: *If you really want to see and know God, you gotta start over, you gotta have new eyes, you gotta be renewed, you gotta be born from above.*

Nicodemus doesn't quite get it, and maybe we don't either at first glance, so the rather confusing and somewhat humorous conversation ensues. Born again? Born from my mother? Re-enter the womb? How can this be? Nicodemus is listening to Jesus the wrong way, and this happens throughout John's Gospel when people encounter Jesus. Nick is listening to Jesus with an old mind. He is not ready for the new mind Jesus brings. Nick is kind of the worst of two worlds: he's a literalist, and he's religious. God help him. By the end of the conversation, it isn't at all clear that Nicodemus has become anything new. And it isn't clear that he understands "eternal life" any better than we do.

This story, as familiar as it is, challenges us to move beyond the familiar, move beyond our old assumptions, let go of our givens and our certainties, and live something new. And this something new, Jesus calls "eternal life." And here's how Jesus describes it: It's like wind and water. Well that clears everything up, doesn't it? That's what Jesus says. Life lived in the love of God now is like wind and water. And those who see God in this life are born of wind and water.

By the way, I'm saying that phrase "wind and water" because in the text the word for Spirit and for wind is the same. So when Jesus says: You must be born of water and the Spirit, it's the same thing as saying: you must be born of water and wind. He even says it himself: The wind blows where it will, and you can't see it or control it. But you can hear it.

That word there for wind is also the word for Spirit, which is also the word for breath: Pneuma. Like Pneumatic or Pneumonia. It might be that sometimes we get spiritual pneumonia and can't breathe in the wind of God very much. To be born of water and wind, Jesus says, is to see God. There's something mysterious about that, and there is something freeing about that. With language that is metaphorical and hard to pin down, Jesus invites us into a life caught up in the freedom of God. And I think the fact that it is hard to pin down is part of the meaning of it. You can't pin down God, but you can live in the freedom of God's love.

And then John's Gospel tells us what that freedom is: God's freedom is seen in God's self-giving love for the world. Jesus is that love made real and visible. And Jesus invites us into the freedom of living in that love, and living out of that love, in and through him.

If you've ever driven through west Texas, or other western states with vast stretches of windy land, you have probably seen them: Fields and fields of wind turbines. Miles and miles of wind energy captured in those amazing, beautiful machines, moving in a kind of grand elegance, a slow choreographed dance. I have driven along looking at all those turbines, and they seemed to be moving themselves. You can't see the wind energy that moves them. But of course, it was there, that free flowing wind, that power.

I have taken several rafting trips in my life, and I haven't enjoyed many of them. I always end up in these super-fast-moving rivers with perilous rapids and dangerous rocks. Once in Wisconsin and another time in Wyoming I was in a boat and felt the force of the river pushing me along and knew I had little control. All I could do was go with it. And when I wasn't convinced I was about to die, I found a few seconds of exhilarating thrills.

Jesus is inviting all who hear him to enter a life caught up in the free-flowing love of God, as free flowing as wind and water. Jesus himself is the self-giving love of God. He makes visible what is otherwise unseen, especially when he is lifted up on the cross. He tells Nick and us that our old ways of thinking and believing won't cut it. Maybe we're like Nicodemus. Maybe we take everything too literally. Maybe we think everything can be managed and understood. Maybe we want to fit God and God's love into our preconceived notions of God and the world, and pin God down like a shiny beetle in our bug collection.

But Jesus says: God is not ours to manage or control or even understand. God is the wind that energizes our lives. God is love that is free flowing like water. Let go of your old ways of thinking and seeing and living. If you really want to see God, you gotta start over, you gotta have new eyes, you gotta be renewed, you gotta be born of wind and water, you gotta be born from above.

If Jesus is God's self-giving love in the world, and we receive that love as a gift to be trusted, we don't do anything to become beloved. We just start there. We are there. So when Jesus says you gotta be born anew, from above, born or water and wind, all I can imagine is we live in the free-flowing love of God, like standing in a cool stream. We trust it, we get caught up in it. It's like opening our arms out like a wind turbine and letting it flow through us and energize us and turn us in a new direction. Like Nicodemus, we might be letting our need for precision and literalism and rationalism and making God fit our world view get in the way. Sometimes, or maybe all the time, we must find a way to let go and trust and let the love of God flow through us.

This is life in Spirit. It is inner freedom to love. It is not just outer freedom where we don't have to live by rules and requirements. It is inner freedom: we stop telling us what to do and we let the voice and flow and wind of God direct us to love in ways that show forth Christ's love for all. When have you felt the freedom of God's love flowing through you so you were able to love another? When has God's love been so real to you that it knocked you over, or pushed you down like a river, or carried you for a ride as you floated along, or energized you like a wind turbine?

In Genesis, we heard the beginning of the central biblical story of Abraham and Sarah. It's a story of God calling our faith ancestors to let go and trust and follow. It's a story of God's self-giving love for the world moving through two small people for the sake of the whole world.

And the text says this one important thing about Abraham when he heard God's call to be born into something new: He trusted God and he went. Abraham opened himself up, he put out his arms like a windmill, and let the mysterious Spirit of God energize his life. Abraham believed that his life could be God's way of making blessing and love and mercy real in the world. It may seem that unlike Abraham, Nicodemus didn't get it when he had his confusing conversation with Jesus. But John tells us more about Nick later, near the end. Nicodemus is one of the two men who show up after Jesus' death with expensive ointments to honor Jesus and bury him and see what God would do next in him.

I know this even if I don't know it with great clarity: Each of our lives has a meaning and purpose in God's world. And that meaning and purpose is found when we sense how it is we have love to give, and we find the newness and power to give it. The power to give it is the very power of the Spirit, the mysterious wind of God that blows through us and energizes us to love. Living in this free-flowing Spirit is utterly freeing, it energizes creativity and innovation in loving, it gives meaning to our lives. Those of us striving to live by faith in God's love in Jesus are experiencing it all the time. We are made new by it constantly. We are born again by it every day. Born from above, born of God, born out of love, born to love.

Jesus says this is how we answer the most pressing question of today: Is there life before death? Yes, there is. There is the fullness of life in God. There is the infinite goodness of God's self-giving love in Jesus. There is eternal life in you now because your life is now one more story of God's self-giving love made real in the world. What else can we do but rejoice?

Incarnation Time Is Here

CHRISTMASTIME IS HERE. . . . I always hear the beautiful, warm, and melancholy chords of Vince Guaraldi's jazz piano song of the same name from the soundtrack to *A Charlie Brown Christmas* when I think about Christmastime. It's a favorite song of mine, and many other folks I think, as it captures something of the spirit of the season in its wide array of emotions.

Christmas means many things to people based on their cultural, religious, and familial experiences and beliefs. One central theme that always comes back to me is the main theological message of the birth of Christ: The incarnation, the in-the-human-flesh reality of God's love. The birth of Christ tells us that God chooses, longs, desires to be in a direct loving relationship with us and all humanity, all creation even. And the way God does that is through taking on the fully humbling and risky birth of Jesus as God's own life in the world.

In the church, we celebrate the birth of Christ as this incarnation, and we also celebrate the real presence of Christ in the bread and wine of the communion meal. We share in the mystery of Christ's presence among us not only as the one born in a manger, but the one who loved the whole world with his whole life, who died for this love, and who was raised to be the ongoing love of God for all. We eat and drink in this love which is Christ and know that God loves us because God is love.

And then we do the most amazing thing: We are sent out to be Christ in the world. We are sent out to embody God's love because Christ is in us. The reality of God is made visible to others through the lives we live in our bodies, lives of service and humility and generosity.

Our world needs good news, as it did in ancient times, and when Charlie Brown wondered what it is all about, and today when so much seems to be going in difficult directions for so many people.

Incarnation time is here. Christ is here among us at Christmas and whenever we share in table fellowship with him. Incarnation time is here, because the time is now for God's love to be real, visible, warm, and touchable in this world. Incarnation time is here. Go play the warm, rich, jazzy chords of living with God's love for others as our primary celebration of Christmas and of all of life lived in God, every day we have left to live.

Rejoice without Shame

Sermon for Baptism of Our Lord A

> Then Jesus came from Galilee to John at the Jordan, to be baptized by him. John would have prevented him, saying, "I need to be baptized by you, and do you come to me?" But Jesus answered him, "Let it be so now; for it is proper for us in this way to fulfill all righteousness." Then he consented. And when Jesus had been baptized, just as he came up from the water, suddenly the heavens were opened to him and he saw the Spirit of God descending like a dove and alighting on him. And a voice from heaven said, "This is my Son, the Beloved, with whom I am well pleased." (Matthew 3:13–17)

It's a new year, and thanks to the festival of the Baptism of our Lord, it's a new start to thinking about who we are. What if I said: Make your new year's resolution to be who you really are more, and less who others tell you to be. Would you know how to do that? Would you know who you are so you can be who you are more? It's not as easy as it sounds. You might have a driver's license, or a passport, or an insurance card, or credit cards, or business cards in your wallet or purse. They all say who you are. But do they really say who you really are?

In Jesus' baptism, God makes clear and visible who Jesus is: *This is my son, the beloved with whom I am well pleased.* This epiphany of Jesus' identity happens for Jesus' sake, and for our own. Because once Jesus' God-given identity is confirmed, he is sent off on the beginning of his mission to serve the kingdom of God, the kingdom of peace and mercy. But Jesus, just like all human persons, must begin by knowing who he is and whose he is: Beloved son of God. And then, he is sent for mission empowered by the Spirit. Identity and mission go together in baptism.

We have this phenomenon in our wired, networked, webbed world. It is called "identity theft." Someone gets a hold of some crucial information about you, name, birth date, social security number, credit card number. Then they go about using your identity to buy this or that and leave you the bill. Suddenly, you are not what your credit report and bank account say you are. Your identity has been stolen. Who are you? And who gets to say? I had some members of my previous church who had this happen to them and it took years to get their records clean and their identities back.

In many ways, identity theft is not new, except in the technological way we know it. For ages, others have been trying to tell you who you are, societies and powers have been giving you your identity. The problem is, you already have an identity, and they are taking it away from you and replacing it with a false one, or a limited one, or a shamed one. Who are you? Whose are you? And who gets to say?

Baptism has everything to do with how we understand our Christian faith. It is so important that at a funeral we light the paschal candle, the candle we light for Easter (Pascha) and for baptisms as well. We do this to remember that a person's baptismal identity is the most defining thing about their life and their death.

Much of our talk about baptism and Christian faith and God and Jesus has been about addressing guilt. We are guilty of doing this or that sin, so God forgives and takes away our guilt through Jesus, through baptism, through a washing that makes us clean. I don't think this approach is entirely wrong, I just think it is very limited in addressing the depths of the waters that God brings us to in Christ.

The real issue, the fundamental problem, is not guilt. Guilt is about what you have done. The real core identity issue is shame.

Shame is about who you are. Or more to the point: Shame says that who you are is not acceptable, who you are is not good enough, you are not worthy to be part of the family because of what you have done.

Guilt for what we have done might make us feel bad about ourselves. But shame for who we are makes us feel worthless, empty, and abandoned. So many of us live with shame, that constantly and only addressing our issues of guilt just makes it worse, not better. People who live with shame, or are told they should, are:

- People who grow up with abuse physical or sexual
- People who live with addiction of any kind
- People who hide their physical or emotional illness
- People who live with perfectionism
- People who have always been told they are not good enough
- People who have been excluded because of their sexuality or their gender
- People who have been rejected because of their race or their nationality or their mother tongue
- People who have been demeaned because of their education level or their social class.

And all of these shames do the same thing to us: They feed us with lies of worthlessness, rejection, and abandonment. They rob us of our true identity. They are spiritual identity theft.

So a whole lot of us could use a spiritual version of LifeLock. LifeLock is a service to help prevent your identity theft. It monitors your credit, looks for your identity data on web sites, and alerts you of suspicious activity. I'm not a representative of LifeLock or know how well it works, but the idea of it gives some sense of security.

The good news of God in Christ is our LifeLock. Who are you? Whose are you? Listen to the divine words spoken to Jesus at his baptism: *This is my son, my beloved son. He pleases me because of who he is, even before he does anything.* This is where we should start. We have to hear that because of Jesus and his baptism, all our waters of baptism have been Spirit-stirred to bring us into our true, God-given, unearned identity: You are a beloved son. You are a beloved daughter. You are a beloved child. Who you are is pleasing to God, even before you do anything.

If only we could get beyond our fear of being who and what we really are! And yet, what Jesus' baptism, and his whole life and death and resurrection says to us is: Get beyond your fear and shame based identity! Be the beloved you are! Know your true identity! Put away your wallet and your driver's license and your credit cards and your insurance cards and your social security card and your passport and your private club membership and your business card and your race card and your political party card and even your Lutheran card or whichever church brand card you carry. Look to God, look to what God has done in Jesus, look to the source of who you are, and know whose you are.

Baptism is where Jesus' true identity was revealed. And in our own baptisms into Christ, our true identity is revealed. It isn't all those false identities we make for ourselves because of fear and shame. And it isn't all those stolen identities that others try to give us as they steal away our true identity in the process. Your true self is the one God created and deemed beloved, and your belovedness has been redeemed again and again, whenever you lose your identity, and lose your way, whether lost by your own actions or what someone else has done to take it away.

Your false self is the one you protect and defend, the one that your compare to others and evaluate, the one that you fill with pride because the shame is so great, the one that separates you from others and makes you shame them. Your true self is simply yourself in God, naked, free, open, human, fearless, connected to all humanity, and above all, beloved. There is no shame in who you are, because of whose you are. This is the power of God's good news in Jesus: You are beloved, son and daughter and child. Now go live it.

In baptism, God tells you who you truly are, but to get there, your false self must die with Christ so your true self can live. More than a washing ritual, baptism is a drowning ritual, where God says: It's OK to let that false self die. It never was you anyway. You are always and only who you are in my love and grace.

We baptize children and adults as God calls them to the waters of the font. God speaks words of belovedness to each, and we are witnesses and sponsors and family. And no matter the age of the newly baptized, that means we have a job to do. We have a vital, easily taken-for-granted job to do: To be their LifeLock! To be the constant reminder and witness to each that they are beloved, and no one and nothing, not even themselves, can take that away. It is not easy to raise a child in this world. It is harder still to raise a child to be spiritually whole and healthy, to know his or her true identity in God, to live with such faith that they have love overflowing for others, they can serve the world in their unique way without fear or shame.

We are a LifeLock for each other and for all who join in this crazy mission we call the kingdom, where everyone is welcomed into their belovedness in Christ, where we try as best we can to mirror that belovedness for everyone. Praise God for Christ revealing the true identity of everyone through his baptism, life, death, and resurrection: We are God's beloved living free, living for God, living of love for others as best we are able.

Rejoicing with Refugees

It was the Monday before the executive order came from the President, the one known as "the Muslim ban," the travel order that immediately stopped persons from entering the United States because they were traveling from one of seven nations identified as potentially dangerous. None of the airport chaos that ensued had happened yet. None of the spontaneous protests around the country had occurred. We knew something was coming, but didn't know when or what or how.

I got the phone call Monday afternoon from a representative from the Refugee Council USA, asking if we could host an event the following Monday. It was to be a modest prayer vigil with presentations by leaders from several refugee settlement agencies. They thought maybe 50 people might come, 100 tops. I checked the church calendar and my own schedule. It looked fine. I said yes.

My heart has long been open to refugees. The most formative experience I had as a youth growing up in the Lutheran church, more than worship, or confirmation, or camp, or raising money for UNICEF, was when my congregation sponsored a refugee family from Viet Nam in 1979. At the time, thousands and thousands of "boat people" were fleeing miserable lives and persecution in post-war Viet Nam. The United States greatly increased its refugee allowance, and refugee settlement agencies like Lutheran Immigration and Refugee Services worked to find communities where refugees could start their lives over.

The family that our church helped settle included 3 adult children and their parents. They had come through several years of harrowing struggles, although they would not speak of them often. After they got settled into a modest rent house, our youth group went by to greet them and bring housewarming gifts. Their gratitude poured out of them through endless smiles and thank yous, which was about all the English they could handle at that time.

During the coming months, my church friends and I began visiting the refugee family once or twice a week after school. We answered their questions about English and American culture. They taught us some Vietnamese words and we struggled with getting the intonation correct. We shared our youthful, joyful acceptance of them. They shared food from their kitchen, much of which we could not identify but we ate with gratitude.

This experience of welcoming, helping, loving, and learning from this refugee family taught me more about my Christian faith than almost anything else before or after. It shaped my life and faith. It showed me that this is what love looks like. This is what church is: we welcome one another, we help the vulnerable, we come through burdens together, and we celebrate new life when it comes. My heart is wide open for refugees from any land, and I am not ashamed to say that.

After I agreed to host the refugee vigil, things quickly got more interesting. The administration's travel ban came out on Friday night. By Saturday, people were stuck in limbo in airports trying to return to the U. S., with family members only feet away waiting for them in anguish. Some people were being returned to where they come from on later flights. Some of those person's lives were at risk because they had assisted the United States military as translators. Visa holders returning to work, teach, or be students again after a holiday break were suddenly finding their lives being shut down.

What seemed the most arbitrary and cruel of the travel ban's restrictions was the prohibition on refugees entering the country for 120 days. Many refugees were waiting to enter in the coming days, with churches and communities preparing apartments and warm, welcoming baskets of food for them. Many were escaping years of squalor in camps after fleeing nightmarish wars and oppression in their homelands. And now their dreams of finding a place to start their lives over in relative peace were being crushed.

Millions were stirred up by this chaotic injustice. The protests at airports across the nation were an inspiring message of resistance by citizens who cared about something more than themselves. People felt energized to do something.

Our already planned refugee vigil that looked like a small event quickly gained interest throughout the community. Hundreds of people were calling the church and the Refugee Council USA looking to attend. All the local press outlets called and planned to be there. By Sunday afternoon we considered whether the event should be moved since our sanctuary can only accommodate about three-hundred people at the most, and that only with extra chairs added on the sides. But it was getting late to switch, so we decided to keep it at the church as planned and try to manage the crowd.

People arrived an hour early. A half hour before the start time, the sanctuary was nearly filled. A line formed outside and went around the block. We guided people into the overflow seating. At fifteen minutes before the start, we let some people stand in the side aisles. Then people began to sit on the floor in front of the pews and on the sides. We had to start turning people away. We were already beyond capacity and while I was making sure doors were not blocked, I was concerned a fire marshal might shut us down. At least we were not planning on a candle light vigil. Aside from the overcrowding, it was very moving and encouraging to see so many people show up to support and speak out for refugees.

Many people spoke during the one hour event. I opened with sharing my story about working with refugees as a youth and the long history of the Lutheran Church working with refugees, and then I led a prayer and a litany. Several speakers from refugee agencies shared information about their work and pleaded for the White House to end the travel ban and return to the refugee settlement policies already in place. Then, a Syrian family that had been settled in Austin for just three weeks came up to speak. Father, mother, and two young daughters gathered at the microphone. After the father shared some of their story, how he lost his factory in Damascus and they fled for years to another country before coming to Austin, the older daughter, just eight years old, began to speak. She was barely tall enough to be seen over the podium even while standing on a chair. She spoke beautiful English, and simply said in her wonderful, young way: Thank you.

The crowd was in tears and stood to applaud. Cheers and clapping went on for a while, and the Syrian family was clearly moved. They suddenly saw that after going through turmoil and uncertainty and suffering in Syria and refugee camps, and after seeing the United States government speak about people like them as some kind of enemy to be feared, they saw that they were welcomed here. They saw for the first time, they said, that Austin was now their home. When you see that kind of deep gratitude in someone's eyes, all you can do is rejoice.

The event was all over the evening news and the newspaper web sites. Over the next few days we got a few ugly phone calls at the church, but mostly, we got thank yous from church members, local citizens, and refugees. "Thank you for hosting this event. We needed to do this so that messages of hate and intolerance don't drown out the love. I'm so proud of our church for speaking out."

What happened that night was a beautiful testament to what I learned when I was in eighth grade helping my Vietnamese friends learn some English and know they were loved: This is what church is. This is what church does. We help people in need. We love people when they are struggling. We don't fear refugees for where they came from, we rejoice with them for receiving the chance for new life in a new home with us, their new neighbors. It's just who we are, and if I learned nothing else about the good news of Jesus, at least I learned that. I imagine that sometime soon as we grow in faithfulness in these demanding days, when people hear about the church, they will say: Oh, that's the people who help refugees. That's just what they do. That's who they are.

Rejoicing from Table to Table

If I asked a room full of people, "What is the church?" I would likely get many varying answers: A community of people who share faith in Christ. An institution that carries the faith on over the centuries. A sacrament of Christ's body for the world. In the Lutheran tradition, the question about what the church is is answered in the Augsburg Confession like this: The church is the assembly of the faithful where the good news is rightly preached and the sacraments are rightly administered. In other words, the church is a good news gathering.

In the tradition of the church, Sunday is a feast day, a day to celebrate the good news of Christ's death and resurrection. It is a day to hear the good news preached and to celebrate the Lord's Supper. In many ways, this simple gathering of sharing the good news of Christ in word, and then sharing the good news of Christ in bread and wine, defines the church. It isn't a reductionist way of defining the church; the church is and does a lot more. But it is essential, and in many ways, it reveals everything. The church is a celebration of the good news of Christ through hearing good news, and through table fellowship with Christ.

The church most often calls its sharing of the Lord's Supper *eucharist*. We might translate this the *good thanksgiving*. While in some times and places this has been lost in the church's practice, this eucharistic gathering is a celebration at its heart. It is a rejoicing in good news that overwhelms and surprises us even as it feeds and nourishes us. Often the church in its poetic eucharistic prayers struggles to find words that express the humble and heart-felt rejoicing that it feels in preparing and sharing this meal of Christ's self-giving love. Perhaps of all the phrases in the many eucharistic prayers that strive for such appropriate praise and gratitude, this one captures it best: *We give you thanks, not as we ought, but as we are able.*

Table fellowship is central to understanding the Christian Gospel, but you can almost miss it. Jesus breaking bread and pouring wine as a sign and seal of his own self-giving love is our defining meal. We also remember all the meals Jesus shared with sinners and outcasts. We cherish his feeding of the hungry and his invitation to his enemies to dine with him. We ponder the stories of Jesus in his resurrected life appearing as a stranger to some forlorn disciples, suddenly revealing himself in the breaking of the bread, and then disappearing. We puzzle over his fish breakfast on the lakeshore with his old fishing friends.

The church in many ways exists as a series of table fellowships. Whether the sacramental table, or the Sunday coffee and donuts gathering, we are brought together by God's hospitality made tangible in the church's hospitality. Whether a communal potluck or a shared meal with the hungry in the neighborhood, we celebrate that God brings us together to be fed and loved as one people.

It might be that the church's most potent ministry in our time when people are dividing themselves up along social, political, racial, class, and national lines, is to be more and more a community of table fellowship. This can happen at churches and in homes, in restaurants and in pop up events that surprise. While the cultural sense of fear of the other grows, the church invites the other to sit down and have some fried chicken and chat. When some groups vocally reject being neighborly towards others, the church hosts a block party and gets people to know each other. As compassion for those in need fades or becomes suspect by some, the church throws a dinner party with a reverse ticket scalping plan: Those with the least get the best seats.

Right now, in your neighborhood, in your congregation, in your home, plan a meal. Invite people to dine together, enjoy fresh bread, savor finely cooked meats, and sip fine wine. Let them share their stories, stories of the day they just finished, and stories of the life they are still trying to figure out. Make it a new and major ministry of your congregation: we are going to gather people around tables of rejoicing and celebrate our common humanity together, which is always made real when we harvest, prepare, and share food. The church could become transformative of this cultural moment of division and fear simply by being a community committed to creating table fellowship and simple celebrations of food, family, friends, and strangers together.

We are still hearing about plans to build border walls because one of our borders feels like a threat (the other one, the whiter boarder, feels benign to those who fear the boarder to the south). As our government talks of building higher and higher walls, the church needs to start building longer and longer tables where immigrants (who likely harvested the very food we eat) and refugees, foreigners and native born, celebrate that at the table sharing food and life, we are one. Should the day come when a ridiculously high wall does exist, the church can still gather at that wall, as it has done at other walls, and simultaneously on both sides celebrate the eucharist, the bread and wine, the body and blood of Christ that unite us across all that divides. I don't know if a liturgical catapult or slingshot exists, but I can imagine flinging holy food across that silly wall, witnessing that nothing will divide us. It might be cause for arrest, but it might be worth it.

There are no easy answers to how to be church in this or any age. But this community of faith in good news, this assembly of believers in divine love and mercy, this body of Christ made visible in the world, can always come together and rejoice at the many tables of feasting and rejoicing, until our celebrations are so loud and uncontainable and expansive in their welcome, all will find themselves rejoicing that in God, we are all one.

God Loves. We Love. Everyone!

Something is stirring in the nation, in many peoples, in the church. No sooner did the rise of Donald Trump begin to threaten people's liberties and sense of safety, and no sooner did those who felt empowered to express hate once the man elected to the highest office appeared to affirm those repulsive beliefs, something got stirred. People who had been inactive or marginally active in the public and political realm decided they could not stay quiet, hide behind their multiple screens, and allow what was happening to flourish. They began to renounce, resist, and ultimately, learn to rejoice that they were not alone and they had power to change the direction of the country.

The congregation I serve sits on the corner of a moderately busy street just north of the University of Texas in the growing and vibrant city of Austin, Texas. Even though Austin is frequently seen as a little blue dot in a big red state, a cesspool of secular liberalism to some, a vibrant and accepting city of progressive values to others, we felt it important at our church to speak out. How could we convey that church means loving and accepting people? How could we send a message to anyone nearby that if they were one of the targeted and scapegoated groups of people in the Trump campaign, we were about radical hospitality and welcome to all? We knew we had to do something.

One of the resources a congregation like ours has is a piece of land. Ours is sizeable for central Austin, an area of high real estate values. It is somewhat hidden away from the main avenues through the city, but close enough to unique Austin cultural establishments like the Spider House and Trudy's that we have some visibility. How could we use our land, our location, our voice in this locale? We made a banner.

Through some conversation among leaders and with some creative design of my own, we made a banner for each end of our property that says simply: God loves. We love. Everyone! We thought it was important for the first thing to be God loves, because that is the heart of the Gospel, not us and our progressive values and our imperfect attempts at living the Gospel through words and deeds. God loves. . . everyone. Simple, but newly important to say. Then we wanted to say that we love in the same way God does, which is to say expansively and generously. No, we aren't that good at it, though we try and keep trying to improve. But still, if the church doesn't somehow live the love of God in its own acts and expressions of love for others, there isn't much there, there.

So we made the banner you see at the end of this chapter. As you can see, it says a bit more. We learned years ago that you can't say God love everyone, and we do, too, and expect people to believe it. People who have heard explicit and implicit messages of rejection by the church (and they might assume, by God) will not find such generic messages believable. The Gospel message of love and mercy is always specific. It is always a message about and for particular people. If you don't say the particulars, then those particular people who have been excluded will simply hear: not me.

Our congregation learned this over twenty-five years ago when it decided to be a church that publicly affirmed and welcomed LGBTQ persons. This was a bold and uncommon step for a congregation to take in the late 1980's, especially in Texas, even in hippy-dippy Austin. But in taking this step, we learned quickly that because gays and lesbians had specifically been excluded from churches and condemned, they needed to be specifically welcomed and affirmed. Many churches want to say they are welcoming, but don't see a need to make a public statement of welcome to anyone in particular, especially if it is controversial to do so. We did it, and it has made a significant difference in the life of people who found for the first time a faith community that loved and accepted them.

It also made a significant difference in the life of the congregation. We were able to rejoice that God's love was known through us and our ministry. The point wasn't to make us look great, although we all fall into that trap. The point was to make God's love in Christ known and transform lives. Like Jesus' parables of lost things that are found and celebration follows, we celebrated this is who God had formed us to be.

When it came time for the banner, we knew that particulars mattered. Who was hearing in loud and powerful ways that they were not welcomed in American society, that they were the cause of our problems, that they needed to be excluded? Muslims, Mexicans, immigrants, refugees, Latinos, women, and yes, still, LGBTQ persons. So we made the banner with all the specifics we thought mattered today.

The banners have been on our property since the month after the election. Pictures have been posted on Facebook and Twitter. Members of the congregation support and rejoice that we can speak such a word of welcome. We also feel challenged to live up to it, and seek new ways of being allies with marginalized groups. When we hosted the refugee vigil that ended up being on the local news, one news station used the image of our banner during a voice over. There it was on local television: the Gospel in particular. Someone added to our banner in bright yellow marker "Basquatch." God loves Basquatch, the illegitimate son of the mythic Sasquatch. We kept it. Humor helps in these often humorless days.

As the confusion and uncertainty and need for speaking out and acting continues in these early days of the Trump administration, and in any presidential administration and any age, we continue to renounce what we must, resist actively and openly, and we rejoice. We rejoice that the church still witnesses to the Gospel and lives are changed. We rejoice that hope is still born in this world that crushes the hopes of too many. Most of all, we rejoice in the God who calls, gathers, and enlightens us in the church, so that somehow through our lives, love goes from being an abstract idea to a lived, incarnate reality that may take all we have to give, but how wonderful it is to be able to give it. God loves. We love. Everyone! Rejoice!

Muslims
Refugees
Mexicans
Persons with Disabilities
Conservatives
Immigrants
Women
Black Lives

GOD LOVES. WE LOVE.

Everyone!
Children
Indigenous Peoples
LGBTQ Friends
Jews
Men
FIRST ENGLISH LUTHERAN CHURCH
Latinx
Liberals
www.felcaustin.org

Scripture Index